GROUP COUNSELING WITH JUVENILE DELINQUENTS

SAGE HUMAN SERVICES GUIDES

A series of books edited by ARMAND LAUFFER and CHARLES D. GARVIN. Published in cooperation with the University of Michigan School of Social Work and other organizations.

A **SAGE** HUMAN SERVICES GUIDE **65**

GROUP COUNSELING WITH JUVENILE DELINQUENTS

The Limit and Lead Approach

Matthew L. FERRARA

Published in cooperation with the University of Michigan School of Social Work

SAGE Publications
International Educational and Professional Publisher
Newbury Park   London   New Delhi

For information address:

SAGE Publications, Inc.
2455 Teller Road
Newbury Park, California 91320

SAGE Publications Ltd.
6 Bonhill Street
London EC2A 4PU
United Kingdom

SAGE Publications India Pvt. Ltd.
M-32 Market
Greater Kailash I
New Delhi 110 048 India

Printed in the United States of America

Library of Congress Cataloging-in-Publication Data

Ferrara, Matthew L.
    Group counseling with juvenile delinquents : the limit and lead
approach / Matthew L. Ferrara.
        p.   cm. — (Sage human service guides : v. 65)
    "Published in cooperation with the University of Michigan School
of Social Work."
    Includes bibliographical references.
    ISBN 0-8039-3885-3
    1. Juvenile delinquents—Counseling of.   2. Social work with
juvenile delinquents.   3. Group counseling.   4. Juvenile delinquents—
Counseling of—United States.   I. Title.   II. Series.
HV9069.F45   1991
364.3'6—dc20   91-7627
                                                                            CIP

93   94   15   14   13   12   11   10   9   8   7   6   5   4   3

Sage Production Editor: Diane S. Foster

CONTENTS

PREFACE

There has not been a single point in the history of civilized society where juvenile delinquency has not been recognized as a problem. Although commonplace and deeply woven into the fabric of society, the ill effects of juvenile delinquency are anything but mundane. This is especially true in contemporary society. It seems that juvenile delinquents are engaging in more serious and deadly criminal activity with each passing year. All too frequent are the articles in the daily newspaper describing how juvenile delinquents rob, murder, and rape their peers and adults. There also seems to be a trend for youth to begin offending at an earlier age. For example, not long ago a 13-year-old boy was given a 30-year sentence for stabbing a peer 97 times. Very young children, even preadolescent children, have been reported as engaging in sexual assault behavior. In the face of all this pain and tragedy, a responsible person searches for a way to improve the situation.

Just as juvenile delinquency has characterized the history of civilized society, so has the effort to contend with it. When reviewing these historical efforts, one is left with the impression that the efforts vary between the extremes of punishment and nurturance. Even today there is discussion of how the pendulum swings from a philosophy of "just desserts" to an effort to rehabilitate. As the pendulum swings, so does the political, economical, and administrative support for particular types of programs. Thus the patchwork, inconsistent historical efforts to deal with juvenile delinquency have given rise to a juvenile justice system that is struggling for a consistent, effective approach. Now, more than ever, there is need for an approach to deal with juvenile delinquents that will integrate the varied historical and contemporary influences of the juvenile justice system.

The "limit and lead" strategy described in this book is one approach that attempts to integrate the just-desserts and rehabilitative approaches. In fact, it is a good example of a contemporary research-based strategy that is based upon two tenets.

First, it is recognized that juvenile delinquents hurt people; consequently, their behavior needs to be limited. In this context, juvenile delinquents are viewed as responsible for their behavior. This is very much in keeping with the just-desserts philosophy, which requires that individuals be held accountable for their behavior. This is done on a case-by-case basis in a humane manner using an array of sanctions and interventions including incarceration.

By effectively setting limits and eliminating the delinquent's ability to gratify personal needs, the second tenet of the limit and lead strategy comes into play.

The second tenet of the limit and lead strategy is that juvenile delinquents must be taught to behave in a prosocial manner. It is not assumed that the juvenile delinquent has a well developed repertoire of prosocial skills. In fact, just the opposite is assumed: Because the juvenile delinquent's exploitive skills enable effective coping, there has been little need for the juvenile delinquent to develop prosocial skills. Thus if one merely sets limits and does not teach the juvenile delinquent more appropriate ways to behave, the delinquent has been stripped of the ability to cope. It is only a matter of time before the juvenile delinquent falls back into an exploitive life-style.

This is most evident when a juvenile delinquent is released after a long period of detention or incarceration. While the juvenile delinquent is locked up, effective limits are imposed, and he or she does not harm anyone. If no rehabilitation is offered, the juvenile delinquent returns to the community with the same basic beliefs, attitudes, and personality. The real surprise in this situation would be if the delinquent did *not* return to an exploitive life-style after release. The limit and lead strategy recognizes that, if juvenile delinquents are going to be expected to behave differently, they must be taught the expected behaviors.

While the limit and lead strategy does try to strike a balance between the just-desserts approach and the rehabilitation approach, it is no panacea. There are many factors that mitigate the impact of this approach. Realistically, one must recognize that, even if the limit and lead strategy is the optimal approach, it takes time to have an impact. Unfortunately, in contemporary juvenile justice, it is not always possible to maintain a youth in a program for the necessary period of time. It should also be recognized that not all youth will respond to the limit and lead strategy. While it may be tempting to label such youth "incorrigible," that may be more of a self-serving statement than an objective assessment. It is very likely that the limit and lead strategy is going to be effective with those youth who would not have spontaneously self-corrected but are not seriously disturbed, chronic offenders.

As mentioned earlier, the limit and lead strategy is based upon an integration of the historical and contemporary influences in the juvenile justice system. The first three chapters of this book deal extensively with the correctional rehabilitation literature. In Chapter 1, the philosophy, goals, and mission of the limit and lead group program are delineated. The foundation for these factors is described in terms of the programs and interventions found to be effective when treating juvenile delinquents. A cost-benefit analysis of the limit and lead strategy is also discussed in this chapter.

In Chapter 2, the discussion focuses on the literature pertaining to delinquent characteristics, counselor characteristics, and therapeutic interventions
with juvenile delinquents. It is important to note how the concepts described
in the first chapter are used to develop an understanding of juvenile delinquents as being responsible for their exploitive behavior and as being
unwilling participants in the rehabilitation effort. It is within this conceptual
framework that therapeutic interventions for the juvenile delinquent are
prescribed.

The issue of how to intervene is the topic of Chapter 3. Once again, there
is a confluence of the traditional (e.g., guided group interaction), and the
contemporary (e.g., cognitive behavioral interventions). Such an integration
of techniques is necessary, as the traditional techniques are designed to limit
delinquent behavior while the more contemporary techniques are used to
teach prosocial behavior. This is, after all, the goal of the limit and lead group
program.

Whereas the first three chapters focus on the conceptual and operational
components of the limit and lead group program, the remainder of the book
pertains to program implementation. Chapter 4 describes the orientation and
in-service training program for group counselors. Training modules and a
training workbook (Appendix A) are provided. In Chapter 5, an orientation
program for youth is provided. As in the preceding chapter, training modules
designed to prepare the trainee for the program are included. Chapter 6
contends with perhaps the most important aspect of program implementation—administrative support. The means for establishing and monitoring
administrative support at the facility level and agency level are described.

Much effort has been exerted to ensure that the group program presented
in this book has a strong empirical foundation. Just as important was the
desire to make the empirical knowledge useful to the practitioner. The true
test of the success of these efforts will come as those using this book embrace
the rehabilitation model and implement a group program that offers both hope
and opportunity to the youth in the juvenile justice system, and safety to those
of us in the community.

—Matthew L. Ferrara

ACKNOWLEDGMENTS

Long before a book is written, colleagues provide influence and ideas begin to formulate. I am indebted to George Willeford, Vicki Agee, and Mario Garza for the influence and the ideas that they engendered. For ideas to develop and grow into something tangible, the environment must be conducive. To Ron Jackson, Executive Director of the Texas Youth Commission, I am as indebted as I am impressed with his ability to create an agencywide environment in which ideas become realities.

Chapter 1

GOALS AND PHILOSOPHY OF THE GROUP PROGRAM

Juvenile delinquents do not need a group counseling program to ensure that they adjust to society and have a happy and productive adulthood. Most juvenile delinquents would make a good adjustment and have a good prognosis if they were given an opportunity to grow up in a safe, stable, prosocial environment. Therein lies the problem. To provide the delinquent with such an opportunity is almost impossible.

While it is difficult enough to create and maintain a safe, stable, prosocial environment, the real obstacle exists in the need to allow time for the youth to mature, or grow up. Time is the resource that is so scarce but so necessary for a good prognosis. In contemporary juvenile corrections, a youth is typically taken out of a negative environment and placed in a positive environment for approximately 4 to 6 months. The juvenile delinquent requires more time than this if a positive environment is to have the desired effect. Therefore the challenge is to develop an alternative approach to keeping a youth in the required environment for a longer period of time. Thus arises the issue of programs for juvenile delinquents and, in particular, group counseling programs.

To be useful, a group counseling program for juvenile delinquents must be an adequate substitute for the unattainable ideal of allowing the youth to remain in a program for an extended period of time. The counseling program should make optimal use of the limited time available by using effective techniques, and not lose time using ineffective techniques. Because so many professionals have been trying to meet this challenge for so many years, the professional literature is replete with information about which techniques are effective.

Oddly, our knowledge about how to best help delinquents began with the contention that delinquents could not be helped. Martinson (1974) sparked a lively and emotional debate among correctional professionals when he published a report stating that no supervision strategy or treatment program could impact the long-term adjustment of a juvenile offender. Martinson's basic contention was that "nothing works." This contention became a rallying point for some professionals who argued that correctional treatment services for juvenile delinquents should not be funded. Some professionals even argued for radical noninvolvement, i.e., providing no services for offenders. Of course, when such general and extreme statements are made, opinion tends to be polarized.

Those holding the contrary viewpoint argued that treatment was indeed effective. If treatment was not effective with juvenile offenders, they reasoned, then one must show why or how those offenders differ from all other clients who do change as a result of treatment services. Perhaps the earliest and most noteworthy opponent of the nothing-works contention was Palmer (1975). In a reanalysis of the same data that Martinson had used to conclude that nothing works, Palmer concluded that treatment could impact the long-term adjustment of offenders. For several years, Palmer and his supporters debated Martinson and his disciples. Although the debate was ostensibly based upon scientific study, the language of the debate was colorful and exchanges were often heated.

Five years after Martinson proposed that nothing works, Gendreau and Ross (1979) published a review of correctional rehabilitation outcome studies. This review was the first in a series of publications by these authors regarding the effectiveness of correctional rehabilitation. Each publication made a noteworthy contribution to the debate on treatment effectiveness and each warrants specific discussion.

In their 1979 article, Gendreau and Ross entered the emotional debate regarding treatment effectiveness and tried to impart some objectivity to the discussion. Using an analytic approach, they reviewed outcome studies that dealt with impact of treatment upon recidivism. The analytic approach simply entailed identifying a program as effective or ineffective, and then specifying the components of each type of program. The analytic approach was useful because it could address two key questions: Which programs are effective? and what characteristics are associated with successful and unsuccessful interventions?

The specific interventions that Gendreau and Ross found to be effective included family therapy, contingency contracting, and counseling. The authors discussed factors associated with a positive outcome for each type of intervention. They reported that family therapy was effective with families who were not defensive and not significantly disrupted by the delinquent's acting out. The use of contingency contracting in family therapy was also identified as effective. Skill training for delinquents was found to be an effective intervention, especially training to teach delinquents how to negotiate and criticize. The authors found role playing and guided group interaction to be among the more effective methods of counseling. In their conclusion about the effectiveness of correctional rehabilitation, the authors identified a few general characteristics of effective treatment programs: Clients are matched to treatment, staff members are adequately trained, more than one agency becomes involved in providing services, and multiple interventions are used in a single program.

Gendreau and Ross (1984) followed up with a publication that was not concerned with refuting the nothing works contention. Pointing out that the literature documents the fact that treatment could reduce recidivism among juvenile delinquents by 30% to 80%, they argued that attention should be focused upon discovering why some programs are successful and others are not. Based upon their review of the literature, they concluded that ineffective programs were based upon the medical model, clinical sociological model, the self-help approach, the friendship model, and Rogerian therapy. Successful programs entailed one or more of the following: anticriminal verbalizations, contingency contracting, modeling, clear rules and consequences, case management for problem areas, and the use of community resources. As in their previous work, the authors underscored that all effective programs are multifaceted since "the superiority of any one technique is yet to be demonstrated" (Gendreau & Ross, 1984, p. 33).

In their most recent review article, Gendreau and Ross (1987) tried to accomplish two objectives. First, they reevaluated the nothing works proposition by surveying the correctional treatment literature from 1981 to 1987. Second, they again tried to identify factors associated with successful programs. Regarding their first objective, the authors failed to find support for the nothing works proposition. However, they were able to identify factors associated with unsuccessful programs: use of the medical model; short-term programs; programs with a narrow focus, poorly trained staff, insufficient client-staff interaction; and programs with a focus on punishment or psychopathology and Rogerian treatment principles. Regarding their second objective, the authors were able to expand upon their previous research by identifying factors associated with successful programs. The authors indicated effective interventions include cognitive problem-solving therapies, rehearsal of prosocial behavior, matching interventions to client characteristics, aggression control training, sex offender treatment, and substance abuse treatment.

The Gendreau and Ross articles have certainly been impressive for a number of reasons: They used the easy-to-replicate analytic approach methodology for reviewing the literature, their research has a longitudinal quality, their reviews of the literature have kept pace with the most contemporary developments, and their findings incrementally build a foundation to support and direct those who provide correctional rehabilitation. While their work has been impressive, Gendreau and Ross are not the only authors conducting reviews of the correctional treatment literature. Not surprisingly, some authors have reached conclusions that are different from and sometimes contradictory to those espoused by Gendreau and Ross.

From the time of Martinson's controversial research to present, the efficacy of correctional rehabilitation has been questioned (Sechrest, White & Brown, 1979; Sechrest, 1987; Lab & Whitehead, 1988). Some dissonance is created because these authors reach conclusions that contradict those offered by proponents of correctional rehabilitation. In attempting to understand the basis of this contradiction, it is recommended that the methodologies used by different authors be compared. This can be quite revealing.

For example, two major methodological differences are readily apparent when the Lab and Whitehead (1988) study is compared to the Gendreau and Ross (1987) study. First, Lab and Whitehead use a ballot box method in their literature review, whereas Gendreau and Ross use the analytic method. The focus of the ballot box method is to provide a tally of those programs that are successful and those that are unsuccessful. The focus of the analytic method is to identify those factors associated with successful programs and those associated with unsuccessful programs. Since the focus of these methodologies differs, the conclusions reached by the authors also differ: Lab and Whitehead (1988, p. 63) conclude, "many efforts do not work," whereas Gendreau and Ross (1987, p. 350) conclude, "successful rehabilitation of offenders has been accomplished, and continues to be accomplished quite well." In a very interesting twist, Andrews et al. (1990) reporting on the effectiveness of correctional rehabilitation, cite Lab and Whitehead's work as supportive of treatment effectiveness because more than half of the comparisons made by these authors revealed a positive impact on recidivism.

The second issue that may help explain some of the contradictory conclusions regarding treatment efficacy is that different authors use different definitions of treatment. Returning to the comparison of Lab and Whitehead with Gendreau and Ross, some important differences are readily apparent. For example, Lab and Whitehead include in their definition counseling conducted by police officers, but they exclude substance abuse counseling. On the other hand, Gendreau and Ross do not consider police counseling to be treatment, but they do include substance abuse programs and other specialty programs such as sex offender treatment and aggression control training. With such differences in the definition of treatment, it should not come as a surprise that these authors reach different conclusions.

The foregoing discussion is not an attempt to explain away the apparent contradiction between treatment advocates and opponents. There is probably some merit to the contentions made by each of the opposing sides, but certain changes must occur before this contradiction can be eliminated. A deadlock in the debate over treatment effectiveness exists partly because the field lacks a consensus definition of treatment. Also contributing to the deadlock is that the criteria of a successful program have not been delineated. Addressing these two issues and establishing some consistency would likely lessen contradiction evident in the literature. This could only enhance our understanding of correctional treatment.

Before leaving the issue of treatment effectiveness, one other methodology for evaluating the treatment-outcome literature merits attention. This methodology is known as the meta-analysis technique (Smith & Glass, 1977). It is a statistical technique that compares treatment and control groups by rendering a statistic known as "effect size." The effect size statistic can be translated into a percentile score that indicates the impact of the intervention on the treatment group. This technique has been used to study correctional treatment, and the results are supportive of the contention that treatment is effective. For example, Garrett (1985) conducted a meta-analysis of 111 studies. The treatment effect obtained was .37, which means treated offenders function at the 64th percentile, whereas untreated offenders function at the 50th percentile. As in previous studies, behavioral treatment, cognitive behavioral therapy and guided group interaction were found to be effective interventions. Psychodynamic therapy and interventions based on the medical model were least effective.

Although the literature tends to support the contention that some treatment can have a positive impact on the long-term adjustment of an offender, the question arises: is the effect achieved by treatment sufficient to warrant administrative and fiscal support of treatment efforts? This question shifts attention from the efficacy of treatment to the value of providing treatment services. There are many different perspectives that can be used to determine the value of treatment services.

The value of effective treatment can be manifested in many ways. For the offender who adjusts to society and does not recidivate, the value of treatment can be found in an improved quality of life. For society, the value of treatment is evident when the offender no longer victimizes those in the community and instead becomes a productive member of society. Certainly, correctional administrators can find value in treatment to the extent that treatment helps

	COST OF MAINTAINING	TOTAL COST PER OFFENSE	RECIDIVISM RATE	EXPECTED COST OF RECIDIVISM
UNTREATED OFFENDER	158,635	+ { 183,333 ×	.40 } =	231,968
TREATED OFFENDER	118,146	+ { 183,333 ×	.25 } =	163,979 / 67,989

Figure 1.1. Cost-Benefit Analysis of Correctional Rehabilitation

alleviate the ubiquitous overcrowding so characteristic of contemporary corrections (Allison & Bacon, 1990). There is, however, another surprising benefit of effective treatment that is frequently overlooked: Treatment can have a positive fiscal impact.

Cost-benefit analysis is the process whereby the benefits of an undertaking are compared with the costs to determine if these benefits warrant funding (Wayson et al., 1984). A recent and convincing cost-benefit analysis of treating child molesters will be presented as a model that delineates some of the fiscal benefits of correctional treatment. Prentky and Burgess (1990) conducted a cost-benefit analysis based upon the following: (a) 40% of all untreated child molesters recidivate at some point in time, whereas only 25% of treated child molesters recidivate; (b) the cost of incarcerating an offender for a sexual offense is $158,635; (c) the cost of providing treatment is $118,146; and (d) the cost associated with recidivism, i.e., investigation, trial and victim services, is $183,333. Based upon these data, a cost-benefit analysis of treatment was conducted. The results are displayed in Figure 1.1.

This analysis suggests that on the average, there is a $67,989 savings on each treated offender. If 100 inmates could be treated within one year, then the annual fiscal impact would be $6,798,900. A savings such as this may actually offset the cost of providing treatment and in that situation, the value of the fiscal impact of treatment would support allocation of funds for treatment services.

Taken together, the literature on the effectiveness of correctional treatment and the cost benefit of treatment services provides a solid foundation for those who advocate treatment. While providing support, this literature also offers considerable direction to those planning evaluation treatment programs and services. Based upon the foregoing review of literature, some guidelines for correction treatment services are offered.

(1) Correctional treatment programs should be multimodal. That is, a program should be composed of several treatment techniques that research has identified as effective. Treatment techniques and intervention characteristics of unsuccessful programs should be eschewed.

(2) The treatment interventions that the research would suggest as effective include behavior therapy, cognitive behavioral therapy, contingency contracting, guided group interaction, role playing and modeling, structured family therapy, and case management. Specialized counseling also found to be effective includes sex offender treatment, substance abuse treatment, and aggression control treatment.

(3) The treatment interventions that research has deemed to be ineffective include interventions based upon the medical model, psychodynamic treatment, Rogerian therapy, the clinical sociological model, the self-help approach, and the friendship model.

(4) Personnel factors also impact the effectiveness of treatment. Some factors associated with successful programs include well trained staff, a sufficient number of staff, and matching clients and staff. Also of critical importance is a clearly articulated and unifying program philosophy and goals.

(5) Effective programs employ quality assurance and program evaluation activities to measure treatment effectiveness. These measures provide the basis for modifying and improving programs. Budget justification for treatment services, e.g., cost-benefit analyses, can also be developed using these measures.

Use of these guidelines in the planning and implementation of treatment services helps to ensure that a youth receives the optimal benefit from the services. Use of these guidelines is economical in the sense that they direct the service provider to only employ those interventions that are associated with successful programs. Thus the program can efficiently use the limited time that a youth is in treatment. The most fundamental issue to be addressed when using these guidelines is the structure of the services to be offered and the underlying goals and philosophy. The structure, goals, and philosophy for the limit and lead group counseling program is the focus of the remainder of this chapter.

The limit and lead group counseling program is actually comprised of several different types of groups. This is consistent with the literature, which suggests that treatment programs should be multimodal. Each of these types of groups varies in terms of function and complexity. Although these groups differ, they are interrelated because they occur in the same setting and are often conducted by the same person. Perhaps the best way to think about the relationships of the different groups is to think of a hierarchy of groups mirroring Maslow's Hierarchy of Needs (Maslow, 1962) (see Figure 1.2).

Each type of group addresses an identifiable need or needs. The more basic groups (Called Groups) are designed to satisfy the more basic needs (safety). Groups become more complex according to their place in the hierarchy. To better understand the differences of the various types of groups, the following definitions are provided:

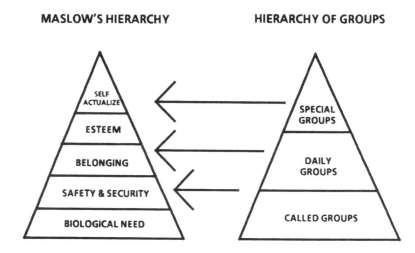

Figure 1.2. Comparison of Maslow's Hierarchy and the Group Hierarchy

- *Called Group.* Spontaneous problem-solving groups designed to prevent program disruption or physical aggression.
- *Daily Groups.* Problem-solving groups designed to help youth develop an understanding of their delinquent and nondelinquent behavior and allow them to modify their behavior so it is more positive and appropriate.
- *Special Groups.* Groups designed to focus on specific topics, e.g., improving self-esteem, dealing with sexual victimization, or aggression control. Youth are assigned to these groups based on common characteristics. The facility administrator and facility mental health staff plan and develop Special Groups based upon the needs exhibited by youth in the program.

Some of the principles that apply to Maslow's Hierarchy also apply to the Hierarchy of Groups. First, one must satisfy basic needs before attempting to satisfy more complex needs. In the group hierarchy, this means Called Groups must be functioning well before Daily Groups will function, and both of these groups must be doing well before Special Groups can be effective.

Second, needs can fluctuate, requiring the counselor to address needs that were previously satisfied. In the group hierarchy, this means that Daily Groups could be running well for a time, and then problems would arise. Staff would be required to deal again with issues or problems they had previously solved. This is particularly likely to occur as there is change in the group membership.

While the analogy of Maslow's Hierarchy and the Hierarchy of Groups is useful, some qualification of the analogy is called for. Consider the following:

(1) Each group actually goes through a series of phases designed to satisfy basic needs (safety) and then more complex needs (self-esteem). Hence, each group can in some ways meet all of Maslow's needs.

(2) Different youth may satisfy different needs in a single group. For example, during a Called Group, one youth could meet safety needs while another youth meets self-esteem needs.

(3) It may be unwise to stop all Special Groups and Daily Groups to simply work on problems regarding Called Groups. Consequently, the group hierarchy is unlike Maslow's Hierarchy in that failure to effectively perform at one level does not totally preempt performance at other levels.

The qualifications regarding the analogy are offered to temper the view of the Hierarchy of Groups. With these qualifications in mind, it is important to understand that a facility's group program is comprised of different types of groups designed to perform different functions. The degree to which these groups are interrelated depends largely upon the degree to which all facility staff endorse and adhere to a well articulated program philosophy. The cornerstone of the philosophy for the limit and lead group program is the program goals. Group counselors, facility administration, and other facility staff must know and advocate these group goals if there is to be a consistent and coherent philosophy.

There are two fundamental goals for this group program. One goal concerns each youth as an individual. This goal is a long-term goal as it pertains to the ability of the youth to adapt to societal norms upon program completion. The other goal concerns the group living environment. This is a short-term goal as it pertains to the living environment in which the youth finds himself, i.e., the facility environment. Each goal will be discussed separately.

The goal for each individual in the group program is to eliminate negative, delinquent behavior and replace it with positive, appropriate behavior. To attain this goal, negative behavior must be confronted and eliminated and positive behavior must be taught and reinforced. This strategy is called "limit and lead" and will be discussed fully later. It is based upon a conceptualization of delinquency which specifies:

(1) Juvenile delinquents have developed behaviors that result in others being hurt (Redl & Wineman, 1951; Yochelson & Samenow, 1976).

(2) Juvenile delinquents have deficits in positive appropriate social skills and behaviors (Goldstein & Glick, 1987).

(3) By emphasizing a youth's strengths and minimizing the weaknesses, a youth can slowly begin to replace delinquent behaviors with appropriate behaviors (Agee & McWilliams, 1984).

In achieving the goals of decreased delinquent behavior and increased appropriate behavior, the individual experiences a number of positive outcomes. First, youth will be better able to meet their needs. Thus the group program serves to empower youth by making them more autonomous. Second, youth who can better meet their needs without hurting others will increase their involvement with others (Glasser, 1965). They will have more meaningful relationships and they will experience increased self-esteem. Third, upon completion of the group counseling program, a youth will be better prepared to conform to societal rules, laws, and norms. Those in the community will be at less risk of being harmed by these youth. These outcomes are the long-term goals of the group program.

In addition to the long-term goal for each youth, a short-term group goal is also addressed in the group program. The short-term group goal is to provide for a safe, stable, prosocial environment in which the youth may change. This group goal is based upon a conceptualization of the group living situations, which specifies the following:

(1) If a youth's freedom is taken away and he or she is thrust into a group living situation, then it is the responsibility of the adults administering the facility to control that group living situation.

(2) If the living environment is not structured and controlled by the staff, then the delinquents will create a group structure and living environment that they know and are comfortable with, i.e., a delinquent environment (Vorath & Brentro, 1974).

(3) Delinquents in a group living environment should be taught and expected to behave in an appropriate, positive way. The youth should reinforce their peers for appropriate, positive behavior, and they should confront negative peer behavior (Agee & McWilliams, 1984).

The issue of managing the living environment is of great importance if the living environment is populated by delinquents. If left to their own, the delinquents will recreate a delinquent environment in the facility. If this occurs, no treatment is possible because the delinquent environment supports the maintenance of delinquent behaviors and may actually punish or negatively reinforce those who exhibit prosocial behaviors. Consequently, the group program must maintain as one of its goals the development and maintenance of a prosocial group living environment.

Based upon the goals of the group program, the philosophy of the limit and lead group program can be stated. For the individual youth participating in the group, group counseling is designed to usher the youth through a series of experiences developed to help the youth have a positive adjustment after program completion. The counselor is responsible for modeling appropriate behavior and demonstrating that one can attain positive goals through hard work. For the group as a whole, the philosophy of the group program requires that each youth help peers in the facility. This includes confronting peers' negative behavior and praising their positive accomplishments. The staff support the youth efforts by making the group program the focal point of the facility program. Facility administrators organize their programs around the group program. Group is scheduled first and other activities are scheduled around it. Relevant information from other program areas is transmitted to group counselors so that it can be addressed. Staff are instructed to not interrupt ongoing group sessions. Group counselors and group counselor substitutes are trained so that there is always sufficient, well trained staff to conduct group.

Overall this book is designed to be a complete guide whereby the limit and lead group program can be developed. This program is comprised of several different components, each with its own function. Properly conducting the Called Groups allows a facility program to establish a safe, helpful environment. Daily Groups help the youth replace delinquent behaviors with prosocial behaviors. Special Groups are used to respond to the specific, identifiable needs of subgroups in the general population, e.g., aggressive youth or low self-esteem youth. The end result of implementing such a program is the creation of a safe facility environment that offers each youth a powerful corrective experience.

Chapter 2

CONCEPTUAL FOUNDATION

This chapter is designed to present the conceptual foundation of the limit and lead group counseling program. The conceptual foundation is comprised of the principles and ideas that guide the group counselor as he or she interacts with the group. Three categories of ideas comprise the conceptual foundation: characteristics of delinquents, characteristics of effective group counselors, and characteristics of the interaction between the group counselor and the delinquent. Each of these conceptual categories is described below.

The first conceptual category pertains to the characteristics of delinquents. The characteristics are presented because group counselors must tailor their interventions to the type of client with whom they work (Beutler, 1979). Group counseling with delinquents is very different from group counseling with other types of adolescents. It is important for the group counselor to know and understand the characteristics of delinquents.

The characteristics of delinquents that are presented in this chapter are based upon two important sources. First, there is the work of Redl and Wineman (1951) with preadolescent juvenile delinquents in a community setting. Based upon their experiences they derive an ego psychology description of the juvenile delinquent personality. Three of the personality factors they describe are listed in this chapter: thinking problems, counter dependency, and internal tension.

Redl and Wineman also offer an excellent description of how juvenile delinquents resist treatment. In the section on Resisting Change and Resisting Group Counselors, eight of the resistance tactics they describe are presented: silence, agreement, rejection, avoidance of responsible people, emotional sabotage, counterattack, double jeopardy, and demands. Redl and Wineman should be credited with providing one of the earliest descriptions of the nuances of the juvenile delinquent personality. Unfortunately, it appears that few professionals in the field availed themselves of this work. It is likely that the treatment technology for delinquents would have been developed to a far greater degree than it has been had their work received more attention.

The second source of information used to describe the delinquent characteristics is the work of Yochelson and Samenow (1976). Although they worked with an adult psychiatric criminal population, much of their work is applicable to juvenile delinquents. They describe more than 50 thinking errors typical of those with a criminal orientation. Of the many thinking errors described by Yochelson and Samenow, eight were selected and included in this chapter as characteristic of the juvenile delinquent: power play, fronting, energy, false pride, responsibility, empathy, thinking, and victim's stance. By combining the work of Yochelson and Samenow with the work of Redl and Wineman, one can begin to recognize some of the specific ways in which delinquents and nondelinquents differ. The purpose of illustrating these differences is to emphasize that traditional mental health techniques are not appropriate with delinquents. The group counselor must modify group counseling techniques to respond to the delinquent characteristics.

The second conceptual category addressed in this chapter pertains to the group counselor. The characteristics of effective group counselors are presented in terms of behaviors that the group counselor can exhibit. An attempt was made to avoid presenting intangible or abstract characteristics. By presenting the characteristics in behavioral terms, the counselor would have a better notion of how to behave during a group session. Some of the counselor behaviors that are effective with delinquent youth are different from those effective with nondelinquent youth (Andrews et al., 1990). If the counselor does not use the prescribed behaviors, the task of conducting group counseling will be difficult. Careful attention to this section is warranted.

The third and final conceptual category pertains to the interaction between the counselor and the youth. It is important to consider the youth and the counselor characteristics separately; however, it is in the interaction between these two that the change process occurs. When working with delinquent youth, the counselor strives to limit the youth's delinquent, harmful behavior while helping develop more positive, appropriate behavior. Thus the interaction between the counselor and youth is characterized by a two-step process: Limit the negative and lead the youth toward the positive. Limit interventions and lead interventions are both necessary for a counselor to be effective.

When building the conceptual foundation of the group counseling program, all aspects of the group counseling situation are considered, i.e., the youth, the counselor, and their interaction. There is little else to consider besides these three components. Each will be fully addressed in this chapter.

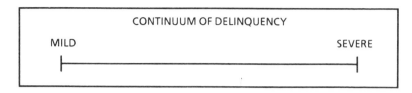

Figure 2.1. Continuum of Delinquency

CHARACTERISTICS OF DELINQUENT YOUTH

It might seem odd to begin group counselor training by describing the client. One might wonder why we are not introducing some other aspect of group counseling instead. Actually, by starting with client characteristics we are implicitly communicating the treatment philosophy: How, why, and what the group counselor does depends upon the characteristics of delinquent youth. This is an important idea upon which other aspects of the group program build. We begin with a definition of delinquency.

For the purpose of the group program, delinquency is defined in terms of one's life-style. If a youth violates the rights of others in an attempt to meet a need, then this youth has committed a delinquent act (Glasser, 1965). If the youth's life-style is based upon consistently meeting one's needs in such a way that it deprives others of the ability to meet their needs, then the youth is a delinquent. Not all youth who commit a delinquent act are delinquents. Only those who base their life-style upon delinquent acts and act delinquent consistently in a variety of situations over a period of time are called juvenile delinquents. Since youth vary in the degree to which they are delinquent, the concept of a continuum of delinquency can be quite helpful.

CONTINUUM OF DELINQUENCY

Work with delinquent youth and adult criminals reveals that they vary in the degree to which they live a delinquent life-style (Yochelson & Samenow, 1976). Some youth only occasionally engage in delinquent acts. Other youth have a pervasive life-style of delinquency. Given the range and variability of delinquency, it is useful to think of a continuum of delinquency on which youth could be placed (see Figure 2.1).

Experience with this population has suggested that those youth who fall toward the "mild" end of the continuum tend to be more impulsive, whereas those who fall toward the "severe" end tend to be more power oriented, exploitive, and predatory (Walters & White, 1990; Zamble & Porpornio, 1988). For the purpose of contrast, two hypothetical delinquents are described. The first one is mild and the other is severe.

- *Mild.* They are suggestible and easily enticed by others or the environment to act irresponsibly. They tend to have difficulty learning from experience or by observing others. Their problem-solving skills are lacking. They act without thinking, and have little ability to handle fear, frustration, or guilt.
- *Severe.* They view the world in terms of winners and losers and are willing to do anything to be a winner. They fail to consider the needs of others. They are angry and have limited guilt, unrealistic feelings of pride, and avoid responsibility.

While it is important to appreciate the different characteristics of a mild and severe delinquent, it is more important to avoid categorizing individual youth. It would be useful to be able to categorize delinquents and prescribe treatment accordingly, but our technology is such that we really do not have an adequate way to accurately categorize. Instead, we must assess each individual youth and determine the extent to which delinquent characteristics are present, i.e., place the youth on the continuum. The more delinquent characteristics a youth possesses, the more toward the severe end of the continuum the youth will fall. The converse is also true. The following is a description of delinquent characteristics that can be used to determine a youth's position on the continuum.

DELINQUENT CHARACTERISTICS

Delinquent characteristics are those behaviors that enable the juvenile delinquent to exploit others and avoid responsibility. These behaviors may be divided into strengths and weaknesses. The delinquent characteristics that help them exploit others are referred to as delinquent strengths. These are not really strengths in the sense that we normally think of strengths because delinquent strengths are destructive. Delinquent weaknesses are deficits in prosocial skills or behaviors. The delinquent has failed to develop these skills and behaviors because the delinquent strengths work so well. The group counselor must recognize the difference between delinquent strengths and delinquent weaknesses because the response to each is different. The group counselor must limit or eliminate delinquent strengths. Delinquent weaknesses must be remediated through teaching, modeling, and supportive interactions.

DELINQUENT STRENGTHS

Power Plays

More than anything, delinquents want to dominate and control. They carry a score card to every situation. In each situation, they "know" that there will be a winner and loser. They always want to be the winner. In fact, they will do just about anything to ensure that they do not lose.

The Power Play is pervasive. It can be obvious as the delinquent exerts dominance during a robbery or assault. It is subtle but also present as the delinquent skips school, breaks curfews, or horseplays with peers. The notion that a delinquent carries a score card should be emphasized. The delinquent expects to always dominate, i.e., be a winner. If the delinquent loses, then attempts are made to compensate by dominating in subsequent interactions with other people.

Fronting

Open communication is a give and take. It is a sharing of ideas, feelings and beliefs. This is precisely how the delinquent does not communicate. The delinquent does not share openly. In fact, openness is equated with weakness. To have a secret is to have control. So, the delinquent shares only part of what is thought or felt. The delinquent's communication can be characterized as full of omissions. It is also one-sided. That is, the delinquent does not take in what others say, nor does the delinquent use the input offered by others. If the delinquent did this, it would be an admission that he or she did not have all the answers. This would surely result in a loss being recorded in the loss column on the Power Play Score Card.

Energy

The delinquent, like most adolescents, is extremely energetic. The high level of mental and physical activity is often used to make life more interesting and exciting. Unfortunately, the delinquent's need for excitement often entails wrongdoing. The delinquent will try to create excitement by aggravating or misleading others. Merely limiting delinquent behavior does not fully address the delinquent's energy problem. The basis of the delinquent's energy is thinking and fantasizing about wrongdoing. Limiting delinquent behavior without addressing the thinking is a sure way to increase the secretiveness and frequency of delinquent fantasies. As delinquent thinking increases, the potential for delinquent acting-out also increases. The role of fantasy and planning will be delineated later in a discussion of the offense cycle. For now, it is important to realize that the delinquent must develop responsible avenues to channel mental energy.

False Pride

Delinquents have tremendously inflated pride, even though they have done nothing to earn it. Delinquents overvalue their uniqueness and insist that others defer to them. False pride can be summed up in terms of entitlement: The delinquent feels entitled to special treatment, even at the expense of the well-being and safety of others. False pride is often present in the claims that life is unfair. Fairness to the delinquent is getting everything that is desired and getting it immediately.

Corrosion

Delinquents do have a conscience, but they also have a special skill that allows them to eliminate their conscience. This skill is called corrosion. It is a mental process that chips away at ideas or ideals which would act as obstacles to crime. It is through corrosion that the delinquent can forget commitments, positive learning experiences, and important relationships that might prevent the delinquent act. As the delinquent corrodes these obstacles, the chance for delinquent behavior increases. It is the process of corrosion that makes the threat of jail time or the death penalty an empty deterrent. The delinquent can even corrode the effects of these severe obstacles.

DELINQUENT WEAKNESSES

Responsibility

Responsibility is meeting one's needs in such a way that others are not prevented from meeting their needs (Glasser, 1965). The delinquent typically refuses to put out the effort to act responsibly. The delinquent is not interested in responsible behavior. It is not exciting enough. Responsible behavior is thought to be foolish and not worth the effort. Merely telling the delinquent to be responsible will not be effective. The delinquent must be taught to be responsible. Responsibility is a skill. It is a skill that delinquents lack.

Empathy

The delinquent developed survival skills long before developing interpersonal skills. Consequently the delinquent's typical manner of satisfying needs often results in others being hurt or exploited. It seems as if the delinquent consistently makes two types of errors: (a) The delinquent does not consider the needs of others, and (b) the delinquent ignores the fact that his/her behavior hurts others. The lack of empathy plays a crucial role in maintaining the delinquent's exploitive life-style: *You can only hurt and exploit others if you don't have empathy for them.* Empathy can only begin to develop as the delinquent begins to look at the past and realize how much others have suffered.

Thinking

When helping the delinquent to change, the group counselor will be amazed and frustrated by the delinquent's limited ability to learn. It seems that some of the fundamentals of the learning process are not available to the delinquent. The root of this problem is probably the various deficits in the delinquent's style of thinking. The following are some of the common thinking problems:

(1) *Failure to learn from experience.* The delinquent does not connect past experiences to present situations. Solutions or approaches used successfully in the past are not recalled in the present. If the delinquent does recall past experiences, he recalls the emotional pain and usually acts out. Thus, the delinquent seems to repeat the same mistake over and over again.

(2) *Failure to learn from others.* Much of what we learn, we learn by observing others. This type of learning seems foreign to the delinquent. The delinquent usually dismisses others' experiences as having no personal relevance. The delinquent seems to be able to circumvent vicarious learning by thinking that what has happened to others cannot possibly happen to him/her.

(3) *Poor problem-solving skills.* Even though the delinquent may have a realistic idea about how to solve a problem, he or she tends not to preplan and weigh alternatives. Jumping into action seems to be more important than planning. Overuse of trial-and-error problem solving seems to be the root of the delinquent's poor problem-solving skills.

(4) *Fragmentation.* Inconsistency in the delinquent's behavior reflects inconsistencies in his thinking. The delinquent's self-concept and world view are fragmented. Although these inconsistencies may be apparent to others, the delinquent does not see them. This allows for competing beliefs to coexist and from time to time cancel out each other. Thus, the delinquent may vow to be kind and obedient, but the belief that he is an important person may allow him to be exploitive. The delinquent would not see this as an inconsistency.

Counterdependent

Most children learn that they can depend on their caretaker for support and nurturance; however, the delinquent has learned something quite different. On many occasions when growing up, the caretaker could not supply the support or nurturance the delinquent desired. Sometimes this failure resulted from the caretaker's weaknesses or deficits. At other times, the caretaker could have been skillful and nurturing but the youth had excessive and unrealistic needs. Regardless of the origin, many delinquents choose not to depend on others. In fact, they go to an extreme and take the stance of a "defiant loner." They choose to avoid intimacy and resist others' attempts to be supportive.

A large part of the delinquent's authority problem is rooted in counterdependence. The frustration which caused the counterdependence is a strong and persistent feeling. When those in authority try to tell the delinquent what to do, the delinquent responds with defiance. The underlying thought is probably, "Where were you when I needed you? You are a little late now. Go away. Do not tell me what to do."

Internal Tension

Internal tension is any unpleasant emotional experience, e.g., frustration, anxiety or fear. Most nondelinquent youth have available a variety of different skills to cope with these tensions. The delinquent, on the other hand, reacts with primitive versions of the fight (e.g., physical acting-out) or flight (e.g., runaway) response. Unfortunately, effective treatment will often create these feelings in the delinquent. Consequently effective treatment is typically characterized by periods of acting-out.

DELINQUENT DEFENSES

Delinquents do not often choose to be in treatment. Instead they are forced into it. To the delinquent who does not view himself as in need of change, group counseling is viewed as a game. The delinquent will try to size up the group counselor and control the situation. The delinquent will try to learn what needs to be said and how it needs to be expressed. He or she will use this knowledge to escape help. As far as the delinquent is concerned, if there is going to be change in treatment, it is going to be the group counselor who changes, e.g., the group counselor will accept the youth. Perhaps the main reason some delinquents have not benefited from treatment is that techniques have not been sensitive to the way the delinquent resists treatment. A large part of the group counselor's success will be determined by the ability to recognize and overcome the delinquent's defenses. The following are the more common defenses used by delinquents:

Resisting Change

The delinquent's defenses seem to be specifically designed to undermine group counseling or any situation designed to bring about change. Some of the defenses against change include:

(1) *Silence.* When delinquents feel vulnerable or cornered, they stop talking. This is perhaps the most difficult defense to penetrate because it does not give the counselor anything to work with. The delinquent usually remains silent until the counselor becomes frustrated and does something that the delinquent can use against the counselor.

(2) *Agreement.* Delinquents use virtue strategically to hide their delinquent desires. Delinquents seem to be able to produce the conformity that adults want, without any change in their motives or goals. Escape into virtue can be very deceptive, but it can be detected. When the delinquent agrees too easily or appears to be too virtuous, it is probably defensive.

(3) *Rejection.* Delinquent groups develop cohesion around delinquent values. Adherence to delinquent values is a matter of loyalty. Those who do not abide by these delinquent standards are ostracized. Thus the delinquent must resist change to have peer approval. This pressure can even motivate the delinquent to act-out just to prove loyalty to the delinquent values.

(4) *Avoidance of responsible people.* In the delinquent's world, responsible people are peers who are nondelinquent and adults who are fair and caring. Whereas the nondelinquent youth may relax upon discovering someone is caring, the delinquent youth must actually increase defensiveness because responsible people are dangerous to delinquent values. Sometimes delinquents can be judged by the company they do not keep.

(5) *Victim's stance.* Perhaps one of the more unusual skills is the delinquent's insistence that he or she is a victim: a victim of society, a victim of alcoholic parents, a victim of whatever. This is one technique that the delinquent frequently uses to try to escape responsibility, especially right after being caught doing something wrong. In taking the victim's stance, delinquents blame others for their own irresponsible behavior. It is the opposite of being accountable. After taking the victim stance repeatedly, the delinquent may indeed begin to believe it.

Resisting Group Counselors

The resistant delinquent cannot be satisfied with defending against situations that could create change. The delinquent must defend against change by directly resisting the group counselor. The following are some common ways that the delinquent resists group counselors:

(1) *Emotional sabotage.* The delinquent tries to distract the group counselor by creating strong emotions in the group counselor. The group counselor who must attempt to quell anger or hide frustration is less effective than the calm, in-control counselor. Ideally, the delinquent would like to get the counselor so emotional that the counselor acts aggressively. When the group counselor acts aggressively and punitively, the delinquent feels justified in remaining delinquent. After all, the world is cruel, especially group counselors, so it is every man for himself.

(2) *Counterattack.* The group counselor who points out a weakness or a problem of the delinquent should be prepared to have the delinquent counterattack by pointing out the group counselor's deficits. In essence, the delinquent tries to

use the strategy "those who live in glass houses shouldn't throw stones." This defense differs from emotional sabotage. In the latter, the delinquent tries to arouse confusing emotions. In the counterattack, the delinquent tries an intellectual assault. The delinquent uses this approach to shift the attention to the counselor.

(3) *Double jeopardy.* Most delinquents seem to be familiar with the tricks of counterargument. They use this skill to avoid blame and guilt. The adult who rushes in and confronts without being able to prove will be rebuffed by the delinquent's counterarguments. Once rebuffed, the delinquent will insist that the adult had one and only one chance to prove the allegations. Consequently, the adult has no right to pursue the matter any further. It is almost as if the delinquent believes that the rule of double jeopardy applies, i.e., a person cannot be confronted twice for a single wrongdoing.

(4) *Demands.* The basic role of the group counselor is to be helpful. The delinquent youth with a history of deprivation may have a long list of previously unfulfilled needs. The delinquent uses this list to make demands that should not be met by the counselor. These demands are unrealistic but can be used to defend against counselors in two ways. First, it can put the positive, helpful counselor in the embarrassing situation of not being able to enact the role of nurturer. Second, it can be used to refute the helpful stance used by treatment staff and prove that these adults are like all other adults, i.e., they frustrate needs; they don't satisfy them.

STRENGTHS OF ADOLESCENCE

It is hard to say which should be presented first: the delinquent characteristics or the strengths of adolescence. In this chapter, the delinquent characteristics were presented first. It is thought that these characteristics determine the unique qualities of the delinquent. Failure to address these unique and not readily recognized characteristics will undermine the effectiveness of treatment. Yet, just looking at delinquent characteristics would render an incomplete picture. Besides the deficits of delinquency, the youth involved in treatment also have the assets of being adolescent. The good group counselor is able to limit deficits and help the youth build upon his strengths. Some of the strengths of adolescence are listed below.

Adaptability

The adolescent has not yet formed a permanent way of perceiving, thinking, and relating. The adolescent's personality is still in the process of development. Although youth may exhibit delinquent habits, these habits can be changed. It takes a great deal of effort to make these changes. Still, change is possible.

Imitation

Adolescence is a time of trying on various identities. An adolescent may imitate just about any type of person or group of persons that he or she is exposed to. In the context of group counseling, this means that the youth may imitate the group counselor or other youth in the group. Consequently, it is important for the group counselor to model the type of behavior that the youth is expected to exhibit. Some of the imitating that the youth does can lead to permanent changes.

Value Development

If the delinquent's values remain unchanged, then the youth enters adulthood with a criminal orientation. Fortunately, adolescence is a time of much development in the area of values and morals. The adolescent is very idealistic, which is a good basis of moral development. The adolescent can adopt the values and morals of those in the environment. Once again, modeling of appropriate values is important. Although the adolescent may ultimately modify these values, it is important to recognize that he or she will "try on" many different value systems before ultimately settling on a fixed set of values. It is important to expose delinquents to prosocial values so that they may be acquired.

Intimacy

For the first time in the youth's life, adolescence brings the possibility of intimacy. The adolescent may be timid and frightened about becoming intimate. Indeed, many adults are. However, adolescents are willing to experiment with intimacy. As they take risks and become intimate with the group counselor, they open up to the possibility of change. This makes it possible and probable for the adolescent to change.

Overall many aspects of adolescence are positive and constructive. When working with the delinquent, it is important not to lose sight of these strengths. It is the strength of adolescence that provides the foundation of successful treatment with the delinquent. Effective treatment always entails enhancing strengths while working around or minimizing deficits.

CHARACTERISTICS OF EFFECTIVE GROUP COUNSELORS

Perhaps the most important thing to keep in mind about counselor characteristics is that in effective treatment, the youth acquires many of the behaviors and attitudes of the counselor. Thus, it is very important that the counselor exhibit appropriate behaviors and attitudes so that the youth can become more positive. In the past, many counselors were taught that the "right" behaviors simply included being warm, empathetic and honest (Rogers, 1957). However, empirical study of this hypothesis suggests that these behaviors are not sufficient to induce change among psychiatric patients (Stiles et al., 1986) or in a juvenile delinquent population (Truax et al., 1970; Ollendick & Hensen, 1979; Kazdin et al., 1987). Consequently,those working with juvenile delinquents must rely on more than just warmth, empathy and honesty. The counselor must develop specific behaviors that respond to the unique characteristics of the juvenile delinquent (Andrews et al., 1990). The following is a list of counselor behaviors that are effective with juvenile delinquents:

(1) *Commitment.* The group counselor must be committed to working with juvenile delinquents. This commitment can be based upon a desire to help youth or help society. The exact nature of the commitment is not as important as the fact that it is a deeply felt prosocial desire. This commitment is important because it will sustain the group counselor through the very trying experiences so commonplace in the treatment of juvenile delinquents. It is the person's commitment that helps him or her rise above these troubles and remain motivated and invested in the work. Youths can generally tell whether or not a counselor is committed. Although they may not fully understand the counselor's commitment, they are often in awe of someone who is committed to his/her work. A delinquent does not typically respect the individual who is uncommitted and is merely collecting a pay check.

(2) *Responsibility.* The group counselor who is irresponsible is discounted by the delinquent. To be responsible, the counselor must meet all his personal and professional obligations. The importance of this cannot be overestimated. The responsible counselor can act as a role model for the delinquent. Many delinquents have rarely seen an adult meet obligations and be successful. The responsible counselor is a sharp contrast to the role models that the delinquent finds on the streets. Since observational learning does occur, being a responsible counselor should be considered a form of teaching.

(3) *Intensity.* Sometimes it takes a great deal of strength and persistence to get through to a delinquent youth. The intense counselor has the strength to penetrate the youth's defenses and the persistence to pursue an issue to closure. Intensity may even be required to gain and hold the attention of the delinquent youth. Delinquents seem to understand and respect an intense person.

(4) *Skeptical.* Believe nothing, doubt everything. This is not a bad philosophy when working with delinquents. The delinquent does front and will tell partial truths or just lie. Since so much of the delinquent's life is based upon deception, the counselor must be skeptical of what the delinquent says and does. Being skeptical entails suspending judgment. The counselor does not

decide if the delinquent has or has not changed. The counselor does not decide if the delinquent has or has not behaved a certain way in a certain situation. All judgment is suspended. The counselor constantly pushes for more information and more honesty. Curiosity is used to probe for more areas of delinquent strivings and desires. The skeptical counselor never leaves good enough alone.

(5) *Leadership*. The counselor cannot take a laissez-faire stance. When working with the delinquent, the counselor must be very directive. The counselor must actively confront delinquent acting-out as it occurs. The counselor must firmly direct youth to address issues important to their rehabilitation. While acting as a leader, the counselor must also know when to back off and let the youth have more autonomy and self-direction. Flexibility is important; however, it is most important for the counselor to be aware that delinquents will require a more directive and confrontational style of leadership than many other group counseling clients.

The counselor's role is basically that of a balancing act. The counselor must be empathetic and honest, but it is also important to be intense, skeptical and committed. This may be difficult because it is not easy to integrate these behaviors which can seem contradictory. Consider two common mistakes counselors can make while trying to enact an appropriate counselor role:

- *Too compassionate*. This mistake occurs as the counselor empathizes with the delinquent's pain and disappointment in life. The counselor may become overly permissive and supportive. Unfortunately, the delinquent views this type of counselor as weak and begins to exploit the empathy. Treatment is not possible as the delinquent loses respect for the counselor.

- *Too controlling*. This mistake occurs as the counselor confronts and sets limits without ever complimenting, supporting or nurturing. In the eyes of the youth, this type of counselor is mean and harmful. Trust is undermined and the delinquent covers up information, thoughts and feelings. Treatment is not possible as open communication has ceased. In fact, punitive, harsh counselors may cause an increase in secretive delinquent behavior.

Naturally, there are more than two types of mistakes that a counselor can make. So it is important for the counselor to self-monitor and correct for mistakes. This requires the ability to self-analyze or accept critique from supervisors or colleagues.

In conclusion, it is apparent that simply maintaining a positive, therapeutic relationship with a delinquent is a difficult task. Like the relationship with other types of clients, the counselor/delinquent relationship differs from everyday relationships. The nature of this relationship requires that the counselor be more skeptical and intense than in other counseling relationships. In return for these efforts, the counselor can expect the delinquent will attempt to resist, exploit and control. Not everyone can successfully form a positive relationship with the delinquent.

INTERACTION BETWEEN THE COUNSELOR AND THE YOUTH

Knowing the characteristics of delinquent youth and effective counselors is important, yet it is not enough to build a solid conceptual foundation for group counseling. In addition to the counselor and youth characteristics, it is important to understand the interaction between the two. This interaction has to be addressed separately from counselor and youth characteristics. Although the nature of the interaction relies upon these characteristics, it is unique and different from them. It is like the old saying, the interaction is greater than the sum total of the parts. Knowing the characteristics is not enough to give you an understanding of the interaction. The interaction is the complex art of counseling; as such, it deserves separate, special attention.

STRATEGY

The basic strategy for intervening with delinquents is "limit and lead." Limit refers to putting limits on harmful behavior. Lead refers to teaching youths alternatives to the harmful behavior. Taken together, limit and lead form an effective strategy for intervening with delinquent youth. The information regarding delinquent characteristics is crucial to the implementation of this strategy. A counselor must target and set limits on the delinquent strengths that are hurtful to others, e.g., power plays. The counselor must lead and teach in those areas defined as delinquent weaknesses, e.g., poor problem solving.

In using the limit and lead strategy, it is important that the counselor does not lose sight of the fact that his client is an adolescent. As such, the client has many strengths, some of which have already been presented. When setting limits and leading the youth toward a more responsible life-style, the counselor must capitalize on the youth's strengths and work around the weaknesses. A counselor must never ask a youth to do something he or she is unable to do, but must be willing to be supportive and nurturing.

The following provides some basics on the limit and lead strategy.

Limit

Setting limits is the first responsibility for those working with delinquents. Delinquents have learned to survive by use of behaviors that often exploit and hurt others. Before he or she can begin to acquire new ways of behaving, the old ways of satisfying needs must be blocked. The caretaker must ensure that the delinquent cannot continue to satisfy needs through the use of exploitive behavior. Until then, the delinquent feels no impetus to develop new behaviors.

Limits must be set so that new behaviors can develop. There are guidelines which can help in limit settings. These guidelines include the following:

(1) *Target behavior.* To the extent possible, limits should be set only on exploitive or hurtful behavior. This effort may be a full-time job in itself. Still, it is important to clearly define for yourself those behaviors you wish to limit. In the preceding section, a list of delinquent strengths was presented. It is suggested that limit-setting begin by targeting these behaviors.

(2) *Clear limits.* Communication is often a problem in setting limits. A youth cannot be held accountable if acceptable and unacceptable behavior is not clearly delineated. In order for clear limits to be set, the youth must be able to explain the limits in words. The simpler the limits, the easier to communicate and enforce.

(3) *Consistent limits.* Rules need not be rigidly enforced. There are exceptions to every rule. Still, exceptions need to be exceptional. To simply allow a youth to get off the hook is to be inconsistent. This undermines adult authority. It also results in the youth losing respect for the adult, e.g., viewing the adult as weak or wishy-washy.

(4) *Firm limits.* If a limit is set or a consequence given, it must be followed through. A limit that cannot be enforced should never be set. A consequence that cannot be delivered should never be threatened.

(5) *Fair limits.* Sensitivity when setting limits is important. The youth's individual strengths and weaknesses must be considered. By carefully setting limits, making exceptions to them can be avoided.

The foregoing guidelines are designed to assist in limit-setting attempts. As evidenced by the guidelines, setting limits is not merely a matter of saying, "no." The entire limit-setting process is quite complex and important. If done properly, limit setting makes the youth amenable to the group counselor's lead.

Lead

In essence, leading entails teaching the youth what to do instead of being irresponsible. Simply setting limits is not enough. If something is taken away (i.e., the youth is told not to do something), something has to be given in return (i.e., the youth must be told what to do). The goal of intervening is to make the delinquent more adaptive in a normal social setting. The goal is not to strip the youth of power and autonomy.

Two important characteristics of delinquents merit attention as attempts are made to lead them to exhibit more prosocial behavior. First, delinquents typically have very poor social skills. It will be difficult for them to acquire and use prosocial behavior. Second, delinquents typically have trouble learning new behaviors. Consequently, it will be a slow process requiring many small steps be taken on the way to the goal.

Just as there are guidelines in setting limits, there are guidelines for leading. The guidelines include the following:

(1) *Positive feedback.* When trying to influence behavior, it is important to use positive feedback, e.g., reinforcement or rewards. Experience has taught us that positive feedback is more potent than negative feedback when it comes to influencing behavior. Frequent and judicious use of praise is a powerful reinforcer. Praise is probably the group counselor's most available and most useful form of positive feedback.

(2) *Shaping.* It is important to break down a goal into its component parts. Every time a youth makes an appropriate step or achieves part of the goal, the behavior should be reinforced. This reinforcement serves as encouragement and an indication to the youth that progress is being made.

(3) *Prompt and fade.* A prompt can be showing a youth what to do or telling a youth how to do something. Initially, the prompt is explicit, e.g., the counselor tells the youth the exact words to say or has him repeat after him. Over a period of time, the prompt becomes less explicit, e.g., instead of having him repeat after the counselor, he is told to recall what to say. Eventually, the prompt is faded out completely.

Although it is possible to discuss limiting and leading separately, it is not possible to properly intervene without doing both. For too long, many a counselor has thought that it is therapeutic to simply limit negative behavior. That is not true. At best, limiting without leading sets up a power struggle between the youth and the adult. Often the limiting of behavior is more designed to meet the adult's needs than the youth's. On the other hand, some counselors have tried leading without limiting. Leading cannot be accomplished without first limiting. This is the type of error that is commonly made by naive adults. They think if they treat the delinquent well, the delinquent will change. Instead, the delinquent views the adult as weak and loses respect for the adult. Alternatively, some adults may think all that is required is to teach the delinquent prosocial skills and the youth will automatically drop the delinquent behavior. Unfortunately, this is not the case. Teaching the delinquent prosocial skills without limiting irresponsible habits only serves to make the delinquent a socialized delinquent. Overall, it is important to both limit and lead. To do one without the other is to do a poor job.

TABLE 2.1   Matching Interventions to Group Behavior

Conselor Intervention	Group Condition
The counselor speaks as little as possible. Positive reinforcement is used to keep the discussion on track.	Group is experienced. Positive group norms exist. Youth can confront and support each other. Youth can problem solve.
The counselor sets limits on negative be-havior and teaches necessary skills. The counselor allows positive youth to model and demonstrate appropriate behavior.	The group is motivated to do well but lacks the necessary skill or is dominated by a negative youth.
The counselor takes charge. Little or no responsibility is given to the group. The counselor is confronting and sets limits.	The group is new or negative. There is little motivation to be helpful. Harmful behavior is readily apparent.

MAKING INTERVENTIONS

Although the goal and strategy of group counseling may be obvious, sometimes it is difficult to know how and when to intervene. Making interventions with the group is the crux of the helping process. The counselor's ability to make appropriate interventions depends upon two factors. First, the counselor must know what types of interventions can be made. The counselor who is able to make many different types of interventions is the one who is most capable of limiting and leading. Second, the counselor must know when a particular type of intervention is appropriate. This is often referred to as the "art" of counseling because it requires a sense of timing that only experience and intuition can give you.

A comprehensive list of counselor interventions will be presented. The list is partially based upon the hypnotherapeutic techniques of Milton Erikson. The interventions are presented along a continuum of limit and lead. Interventions that require the counselor to be active are limiting interventions, i.e., designed to stop harmful behavior. Interventions that allow the counselor to turn over responsibility to the group and let the group do the problem solving are "leading interventions," i.e., designed to develop positive behaviors. Groups that are adaptive and responsible will result in more *lead* interventions by the counselor. The counselor will need to use *limit* interventions with groups that are new or experiencing trouble being positive. Table 2.1 depicts the counselor interventions appropriate for various group conditions.

As can be seen in Table 2.1, the counselor varies the type of intervention depending upon the group condition. Assessing the group condition and modifying the intervention is the "art" of therapy. Ideally, the counselor would like to be able to turn over responsibility of the group to the group members. It is, however, a rare occurrence when a group of delinquents can perform in such a manner. Still, it is a goal worth pursuing. The counselor must constantly be adjusting and readjusting interventions to fit the limit and lead needs of the group.

Having discussed the timing of intervening in broad terms, it is now time to discuss the limit and lead strategy in more detail. To do this we will focus on specific types of interventions. The following list of interventions is presented on the continuum of limit and lead. Limit interventions are used when the group is negative or out of control. Lead interventions are used when the group is capable of problem solving, confronting and supporting. Interventions are made in response to the need of the group at that particular point in time.

Minimal Lead

(1) *Approving.* A response designed to reassure a youth. It reinforces the existing behavior, thoughts or feelings. Be sure not to use it when the youth exhibits negative behavior or you will reinforce negative behavior. An example of approving: "I agree with you."

(2) *Delay.* A noncommittal response or no response at all. This forces the group members to continue talking or doing what they were doing. Once again, one must be cautious, as a delay may imply approval. An example of a delay: silence.

(3) *Closed question.* A question that calls for a yes or no response. The closed question is usually used to make a point or redirect the discussion, e.g., "Are we talking about what we need to be talking about?"

Moderate Lead

(1) *Reflection.* A restatement of an utterance by a youth. It demonstrates understanding and may imply approval. It can be used selectively to direct conversations. Reflections can emphasize the content of an utterance or the underlying feeling, e.g., "If I understand you correctly, you've said that Johnny deserved to be hit because he antagonized you."

(2) *Clarification.* The counselor uses his/her own words to summarize the discussion. It can be helpful if the youth has been rambling. It can be used to provide direction, e.g., "You've touched on quite a few topics, but the theme of concern for others keeps coming up."

(3) *Open-ended question.* A probing question designed to focus the youth's attention on a particular issue, e.g., "Why don't you tell me about other times when you've been angry?"

Moderate Limit

(1) *Developing alternatives.* The basic goal of counseling is to make a change. Change occurs when the youth develops alternatives and behaves differently. Thus, developing alternatives represents a limit of negative behavior. The youth cannot exhibit a new positive behavior and an old negative behavior simultaneously. Thus, the new behavior limits the old. An example of developing alternatives: "Ask the other group members how they've handled it when they've had this problem."

(2) *Redirection.* Refocusing the group to maintain a problem-solving approach or prosocial values, e.g., "We've gotten off the topic. Let's return to the issue of cheating on the exam;" or, "We seem to be focusing on the group scapegoat. Shouldn't we instead be talking about the cheating on the exam?"

(3) *Labeling.* Pointing out prosocial and delinquent behavior, thinking or feeling. This is used to reorient the youth's belief system, e.g., "Exploiting others as you did, Johnny, is always irresponsible."

Large Limit

(1) *Confrontation.* Describing an aspect of the youth's behavior he would like to deny, or verbalizing the impact of the youth's behaviors. Confrontation of behaviors occurring in the treatment setting are particularly strong, e.g., "Your constant laughing and distracting keeps the group from problem solving."

(2) *Interpretation.* Designed to uncover the youth's goals or motives. Interpretations are very powerful; however, it is easy to make mistakes. Interpretations should be offered, not forced. One in-depth interpretation may be all that a youth can tolerate in one session, e.g., "You treat female staff poorly because you're angry at your mother for her neglect and abuse of you."

(3) *Expulsion.* A youth who won't respond to limit setting must be expelled from the session for that day. Any youth expelled from a group must also receive negative consequences. The group counselor should meet with the youth who was expelled and try to resolve any conflicts prior to the next group session.

As can be seen from this continuum, the interventions comprising half of the continuum put limits on the youth's irresponsible behavior. The interventions comprising the other half of the continuum are designed to lead and give the youth more responsibility. As always, the counselor must modify the interventions to match the group conditions. Moderate lead interventions will probably be the most common type of intervention. Ideally, the counselor should strive to use only minimal lead interventions, as this would mean that group members are performing well and making progress.

TABLE 2.2   The Impact of Interventions on Different Types of Delinquents

	Mild Delinquent	Severe Delinquent
Minimal Lead Approve Delay Closed Question	Many interventions will be of this type because the youth requires support and approval.	Used as a staff tactic to buy time to figure out how to intervene. It may be viewed as weakness.
Moderate Lead Reflection Clarification Open Question	Teaching by clarification and reflection is useful. It is helpful to point out their own behavior/ words to them.	Good way to direct but still requires caution. Their words should be used to focus the group.
Moderate Limit Develop Alternative Redirection Labeling	Redirection may be used frequently as they are dis- tractible.	Redirection and labeling may be used frequently as they try to front and con.
Large Limit Confrontation Interpretation Expulsion	To be used only when it can be followed by support. These interventions can cause acting- out.	Used strategically to break up cliques. Good way to keep them off balance and open to change.

INTERVENTIONS FOR DIFFERENT TYPES OF DELINQUENTS

Previously, two hypothetical types of delinquents were identified: the mild delinquent and severe delinquent. The two types of delinquents are contrived so that counselors can better understand and help the delinquent. Thus, the typology is more for the convenience of the counselor than an actual reflection of reality. In reality, a delinquent may fall anywhere upon a continuum from mild to severe delinquency.

Given the individual differences among delinquents, it makes sense for the counselor to modify the interventions depending on the type of delinquent. While flexibility is crucial, so is consistency. Some things do not change. The goal of treatment is still to increase responsibility and positive behavior. The strategy of treatment is still to limit and lead. The continuum of interventions is still applicable. The flexibility pertains to the manner of using interventions. Table 2.2 and Table 2.3 give an overview of how the different interventions might be used with different individuals.

As can be seen in Table 2.2 and Table 2.3, different youth can and do react differently to the same intervention. Becoming an effective counselor requires that one be able to assess each individual's level of functioning and intervene appropriately.

MAKING INTERVENTIONS WITH THE GROUP

Through the years, many group counselors have come to realize the power of the peer group on adolescents. The more experienced and effective group counselors have found ways to use the peer group to help youth change. These group counselors actually capitalize on the fact that they are not in a one-to-one situation. They seize the opportunities that the group setting offers and direct the group influence in order to help.

The techniques for using group influence effectively are quite simple. To the extent possible, the counselor avoids addressing individual group members. Instead, interventions are directed to the group as a whole. The intention behind such an approach is to have the group members do the work. Naturally, the impact is very powerful because it combines two potent components: the group member is interacting with his peer group; and, the group members are using the counselor's influence and direction when interacting with each other. The following are a few general examples of effective group interventions. These are interventions in which the counselor addresses the entire group, not individuals in the group.

Redirection

The purpose of group is to solve problems. Even when functioning at their very best, people tend to avoid problems and may become sidetracked. With involuntary clients such as delinquents, problems are often avoided in an attempt to undermine the helping process. Regardless of the reason, the group counselor needs to direct the youth and keep them focused on the appropriate topic. It should be noted that redirection always amounts to asking the group to talk about something that they consciously or unconsciously tried to avoid. Some examples:

> "When Mario brought out his problem, he admitted he hated the staff. Don't you think we should talk about that?"
> "The discussion is focusing on Brandon's cheating problem. We seem to be forgetting that he recently tried to escape."
> "I know it's easier not to talk about it, but someone needs to ask Gary about his sexual behavior last night."

Process Comments

The group counselor avoids becoming a discussion participant with the goal of observing *how* the group is conducting itself. When the group counselor detects that the discussion is not productive, an attempt is made to determine why, and the group is directed to address the problem. For example, the group counselor detects that the discussion is quite superficial. After watching the group process for a while, the group counselor notices that problems are being minimized. The group counselor then intervenes and asks the group if they recognize the problem. The group counselor then asks the group to address the problem before progressing. Some examples of process comments might include:

> "Do you notice that every time we point out a problem, Jay seems to reverse it and make it someone else's problem? It looks like the group is letting Jay establish the norms. Don't we already have group norms for responsibility?"
> "Do you notice Sandra and Steffany are not paying attention? I wonder if the group is focusing upon relevant issues."
> "The group does a good job bringing out problems, but all Ron does is accept them and say he can change. Doesn't it sound like he is minimizing? I wonder why no on has confronted Ron about this."

Counterattack

The delinquent is oriented toward avoiding responsibility. In the group session this might manifest and undermine the group process. This might occur in any number of subtle and not so subtle ways. A very subtle way to undermine the group process might be to ask the group counselor to explain rules, e.g., "Why do we have to wear shirts to group?" or "Why don't I have more than $5 from my trust fund? It's my money." Besides the subtle diversions, there are not so subtle attacks that delinquents use to undermine the change process. Usually the attacks are direct assaults upon the group counselor. The intention is to make the group counselor defensive, thus enabling the delinquent to escape the change process. Whether the attack is subtle or overt, indirect or direct, the group counselor should respond by enlisting the aid of the group, for example:

> "George wants to know why he can't have more than $5 from his fund. Does anyone want to explain that to him?"
> "Elise is calling me 'mean' and 'unfair'. Can anyone help her formulate a question she can ask me that allows us to get at the problem?"
> "Beth doesn't like using the group format. Can someone explain why we use structure and why we use a group format?"

Responding to a group member by asking the group to respond is one of the more effective ways to use the therapeutic potential of the group setting. Naturally, it will not be possible to always sidestep responding to an individual. Nor will it always be possible to avoid self-disclosure or responding personally. Still, it is best to reserve this type of activity until you offer a summary at the end of group. To the extent possible, stay out of the discussion and allow the youth to help each other. That is why they were put in a group setting.

CHAPTER SUMMARY

The organizing concept of this chapter is that specific interventions are required for specific problems. As an organizing concept, this is certainly not novel. This concept is used routinely in counseling as clinicians strive to link treatment with diagnosis (Beutler, 1979). What is novel is that juvenile delinquency is deemed to be the problem and its specific characteristics are described such that specific interventions can be developed. Many treatment programs have failed because they tried to categorize the delinquent into a preexisting conceptual framework. Pigeon-holing the delinquent into the preconceived treatment concepts of the medical model, psychodynamic approach, or the humanistic approach has not proved fruitful (Gendreau & Ross, 1987). In this chapter, the specific characteristics of juvenile delinquents were described and based upon this description, the necessary group counselor characteristics, and the strategy for intervening with delinquents in a group counseling setting. Every effort was made to maintain the integrity of the conceptualization of the juvenile delinquent when describing the counselor characteristics and the counseling strategy. Continuity among these elements is essential if one is to develop and maintain a cohesive conceptual basis. With such a conceptual foundation, specific intervention can be developed. That is the focus of the next chapter.

Chapter 3

PRACTICAL GUIDELINES

This chapter is designed to translate the philosophy and concepts presented in the preceding chapters into practical "how-to" guidelines. Chapter 3 in no way modifies or changes the material presented in the preceding chapters. Rather, it operationalizes the concepts and ideas previously presented.

The guidelines presented in this chapter draw up some of the more noteworthy traditional and contemporary influences in correctional rehabilitation. For instance, those familiar with guided group interaction and positive peer culture will readily recognize these influences. In fact, the recommended structure for Daily Groups is very similar to that used in positive peer culture (Vorath & Brentro, 1974; Harstead, 1976; Brentro & Ness, 1982). The use of Huddle-ups and Large Groups have their roots in guided group interaction. However, these traditional influences are only part of the foundation of the practical guidelines presented in this chapter. The more contemporary approach of cognitive behavioral therapy is also included. The basis for combining these two influences is as necessary as it is important. Consider some of the research findings to emerge in the past decade.

The recent literature does support the contention that correctional treatment programs can reduce recidivism (Gendreau & Ross, 1984). The literature is clear, however, that there is no panacea and that different types of interventions can have different types of results. Specifically, it appears that programs based upon the guided group interaction principles do not have a significant impact upon recidivism (Romig, 1982). The guided group approach does, however, contribute greatly to the maintenance of a safe, trouble-free environment. Therefore, it is wise to include components of the guided group interaction approach in any facility program for juvenile delinquents. Establishing a safe, stable facility environment is not a goal but it is a means to achieving a goal. The goal of any facility program should be to help the delinquent change in such a way that recidivism is less likely. The literature is clear on the types of interventions that are most effective in reducing recidivism. It appears that behavioral approaches and cognitive behavioral approaches are the most effective (Romig, 1982; Garrett, 1985; Gendreau & Ross, 1987). However, these approaches do little or nothing to create a safe facility environment. When elements of the traditional guided group interaction approach are combined with elements of cognitive behavioral therapy, an effective group program can be developed. The guided group interaction techniques are used to set limits on negative behavior and create a safe, stable environment. The cognitive behavioral approaches are used to teach the youth prosocial attitudes that can result in more appropriate behavior and, consequently, lower recidivism rates.

Because guided group interaction and cognitive behavioral techniques are used, this group program is comprised of several types of group: Called Groups, Daily Groups, and Special Groups. Guidelines for conducting Called Groups are the first presented in this chapter. The Called Group is a method for interrupting negative activities. It is the primary technique used by counselors to manage the facility's milieu. These groups are based largely upon guided group interaction techniques. Proper use of the Called Group sets up the Daily Group to be a powerful, therapeutic experience. The guidelines for conducting Daily Groups comprise the second section of this chapter. The structure of the Daily Group is presented and the emphasis is placed upon problem solving. Conditions that normally arise in the routine use of Daily Group are addressed. Cognitive behavioral techniques are also provided whereby youth are guided through experiences that result in lasting changes.

The final section of this chapter pertains to the design and implementation of special groups. Guidelines for running special groups are not presented since there are myriad possibilities when it comes to the topic of special groups. Instead, a model is offered whereby these groups can be designed and implemented.

GUIDELINES FOR CONDUCTING GROUPS

CALLED GROUPS

There are two basic types of Called Groups: the Huddle-up and the Large Group. Each group is dramatically different although both are used to maintain a safe living environment. The following are the guidelines for these groups.

Huddle-ups

Huddle-ups are brief (10-15 minutes) groups designed to interrupt a destructive activity. In extreme situations, the purpose is to avoid a physical confrontation between two youth or between staff and youth. In most situations, the Huddle-up serves to preempt program disruption. In simply initiating the group and stopping the negative activity, a counselor has accomplished a large part of the task. It is important to remember that a Huddle-up is just one tool available to staff who want to interrupt a negative activity. It should, however, be the primary tool used by counselors.

Recognizing the Need for a Huddle-up. There are four situations in which the use of a Huddle-up is one appropriate way to intervene. When a counselor determines that one of these situations exists, a Huddle-up may be conducted. The four situations are:

(1) Overt aggression or the threat of overt aggression
(2) Flagrant violation of the rights of others and no sign of stopping in spite of staff confrontation
(3) Escape or attempted escape
(4) Serious challenges to staff, which may lead to a physical confrontation

Huddle-ups are primarily designed to help counselors avoid confrontations that might result in a restraint or an assault. The four situations warranting a Huddle-up are those that often result in physical confrontation. Huddle-ups are designed to circumvent these confrontations by shifting the focus of the problem. For example, if a youth is challenging the authority of the counselor, the counselor could call a Huddle-up. The focus then shifts from the counselor/youth interaction to the interaction between the youth and his peers. In this way, the counselor can sidestep a confrontation and possibly prevent a restraint.

Initiating a Huddle-up. Only staff may initiate a Huddle-up. Although a youth may request a Huddle-up, it will always be the responsibility of staff to call and conduct a Huddle-up. If youth are allowed to initiate Huddle-ups, the potential for abuse would be hard to control. For example, a youth could seek revenge on another youth by initiating a Huddle-up. Or, a youth could interrupt a scheduled activity by initiating a Huddle-up. To avoid these problems and others, only staff initiate Huddle-ups.

The essential element in deciding to initiate a Huddle-up is timing. Staff must know the youth who comprise the group. A staff person must have a sense that there are positive youth in the group and that these youth would be willing to confront a negative peer. If the staff does not sense that this support is available, then another tactic should be employed, e.g., call for extra staff to assist with the situation.

The youth participating in the Huddle-up should stand or sit in a circle. The youth having a problem should be near the counselor. Youth who are angry with each other should never be placed right next to each other or directly across from each other. This can intensify the anger and could lead to physical aggression. No one is placed in the center of the circle. This is a technique that has been used in the past, but it has no therapeutic benefit. In fact, counselors who place a youth in the center are probably just acting out their anger and control issues.

The location of the Huddle-up depends upon where the group is at the time of the incident. Huddle-ups are spontaneous and, consequently, may be conducted just about anywhere. The primary constraint put on the location of the Huddle-up is that it should be relatively free of distraction. For example, if the incident occurs in the cafeteria, all should move outside the cafeteria. Other issues regarding location that warrant attention include:

(1) Counselors must not allow the problem person to stand or sit next to a door.

(2) The group must move out of any area where there are breakable objects (e.g., glass) or objects that can be thrown.

(3) The chosen location should be physically comfortable, i.e., youth should not be forced to endure harsh environmental conditions.

(4) Counselors are not to conduct the Huddle-up in an open space that may allow the youth to run away.

Finally, the counselor should be careful as to how the Huddle-up is announced. The youth in the group will mirror the tone set by the counselor. It is best to maintain a matter-of-fact tone and communicate to the youth that everyone should be objective and fair.

Structure of the Huddle-up. The structure of the Huddle-up is comprised of a three-step problem-solving process: The problem is identified, responsibility for the problem is assigned, and alternatives are developed. The entire problem-solving process can be conducted quickly since there is no attempt to do therapy or analyze the youth. Quick resolution is important because the goal of the Huddle-up is to solve problems and prevent program disruption. Each step in the problem solving process is discussed below.

(1) *Identifying the problem.* The first objective is to establish that a problem exists. Ideally, the youth with the problem should state exactly what problem exists. Although a youth may know what problem exists, often there is an unwillingness to admit to the problem. In this case, the counselor must identify the

problem for the youth and group members. In order to identify a problem, the counselor who convened the group must give a behavioral description of the problem. A behavioral description includes:

- Who—the persons involved
- What—a step-by-step account of what happened
- When—the time of the event
- Where—the location of the event

Identifying the problem does not include "why." If you get into this issue, you will be talking about the youth's motives and goals. These are not at issue in a Huddle-up, although this may be very much the focus of a Daily Group. Rather, the focus is exclusively on the behavior because the purpose of the Huddle-up is to prevent program disruption so that the normal facility routine can be followed.

An important part of identifying the problem entails having the group affirm that a problem exists. When a youth's peers confront him about a problem, it is more powerful than when an adult does. You can generate this peer pressure by involving the other youth. This is accomplished by:

- Asking other youth to describe the problem, if they observed it
- Asking the group to explain why the behavior is a problem

(2) *Assigning responsibility.* After identifying the problem, the counselor must let the youth know that he/she is responsible for that behavior. Naturally, the youth will want to deny the behavior or explain it away (rationalize). The counselor should use the peer group to keep the youth from avoiding responsibility. It is very important that the youth be held accountable for his or her problem. The youth may not be able to accept responsibility for the problem behavior. It is important not to get bogged down on this issue. Simply getting the youth's attention and assigning responsibility may be all that can occur in the Huddle-up. The responsibility issue can be followed up in the Daily Group.

(3) *Develop alternatives.* This is actually an abbreviated form of goals setting and planning. The leader must direct the group through several steps of the problem-solving process.

- The troubled youth is informed that the problem behavior is not acceptable and that some other behavior must be used to meet his goals. (Note: This statement is based upon the limit and lead strategy.)

- The group and the youth develop a goal. The goal usually pertains to what the youth hoped to accomplish when the problem behavior was exhibited. The goal developed in the Huddle-up may be no different than the youth's original goal that started the negative behavior. What may differ is the plan. On the other hand, some youth do have unrealistic goals. In this case, the youth would have to come up with a new goal.

- The group develops plans or suggests alternative behavior so the goal could be obtained. The counselor should be willing to allow the group to develop and entertain various plans. The counselor provides guidance and helps to ensure the group's success in meeting its goals.

- Have the youth commit to the plan.

When working with the Huddle-up, it is important to use the principle of "successive approximations." That is, the counselor must have high expectations for the youth but move in small increments toward these high expectations. When appropriate behaviors are exhibited, one should reinforce the youth.

(4) *Concluding the Huddle-up.* The counselor should have a clear-cut criteria for concluding the group. The leader should know this criteria even before calling the group and should keep the criteria in mind throughout the Huddle-up. The counselor also needs to give consequences to the youth who had the problem. The consequence does not have to be severe but must occur. The purpose of giving consequences is to reinforce the notion that a youth may earn reward or punishment depending on the type of behavior exhibited.

Of course there are times when it is not possible to have a constructive group. If the counselor detects that the group cannot meet an appropriate concluding criteria, then the end of the group should be delayed. Some indications that a delay is necessary may include:

- The group is verbally attacking the troubled youth or sermonizing without listening to him or her.
- The youth are using group to vent anger at each other, e.g., playing get back.
- The youth are forcing an inappropriate solution.
- There is a great deal of lying or fronting, i.e., trying to say the right thing without meaning it.

If a delay is required, then the group must receive negative consequences for the failure. All the youth in the program must be taught that there are consequences for all behaviors. Negative consequences occur in response to negative behaviors.

At other times, the session may require more than the 15 minutes allotted to a Huddle-up. A leader may extend the time of a session if and only if:

- The troubled youth has admitted to the problem.
- The group is providing positive input.

When concluding the group, the counselor is responsible for summarizing the events of the group. The summary should include:

- Restatement of the problem or the reason for the group
- Explanation of why the problem did not fit the activity
- Restatement of the solution and the youth's commitment
- Reinforcement of positive individuals or positive group performance

There are many constraints placed upon the Huddle-up. It should be a brief, problem-solving group. Despite the outward appearance of being simple, the leader must actively direct the group and provide the structure for problem solving. The apparently simple outward appearance does not reflect the actual complexity of this type of group.

Large Groups

Large groups are problem-solving groups that involve all youth assigned to a specific living environment. The group begins when staff call together all the youth in response to serious and sometimes life-threatening situations. The Large Group is designed to uncover these serious situations and may be conducted for several hours at a time. The purpose of the Large Group is to prevent activity that may result in others being harmed.

Recognizing the Need for a Large Group. The following are the reasons for calling a Large Group:

(1) Staff know that a weapon is in the living environment, i.e., dorm, cottage or halfway house.
(2) Staff know that a tool which could be used for escape is in the environment.
(3) An escape plan or an assault plan has partially surfaced.
(4) There are pervasive problems in the group which began to appear in the form of physical or sexual assaults.
(5) Contraband is present.

In general, a Large Group is conducted in response to threats to the physical welfare of staff and youth. Naturally, attempts should be made to determine which youth are involved in these serious situations. Ideally, the counselor would like to work with these youth in a Huddle-up. Sometimes, however, the problem is too widespread. Many youth may be involved. Other youth may be subjected to threats and intimidation. In this situation, the Large Group is the only method which holds much promise for remediation.

Conducting a Large Group. Large Groups are problem-solving groups designed to resolve issues that affect all persons in a living environment. Thus all youth and all available staff must participate. The following are guidelines for conducting a Large Group:

(1) The entire group process is preplanned. All staff must agree beforehand on the goals and the strategy to be used during the group. It is important to specify the exact information or action that will be the goal of the Large Group. It is also very important to plan for possible negative contingencies, e.g., assaults or restraints.

(2) Everyone in the cottage assembles. Youths should be seated in chairs forming a circle or semicircle. The staff person conducting the group should sit in the group. Other staff may sit in group or stand outside the circle. All staff should participate and be ready to respond to the youth.

(3) The issue to be resolved is introduced. Use of the basic problem-solving process typically used in a Huddle-up is implemented. Much emphasis should be placed upon identifying the problem—determining the who, what, when and how of the problem.

(4) Group members must be kept focused. Large Group is conducted for extended periods of time. It is important that the group members not get sidetracked. Youth who daydream or distract are to be confronted. Some youths will try to "check-out" of the Large Group by behaving in a manner calculated to result in their being restrained or sent to security/detention. The counselor or staff will avoid playing into this manipulation and try to keep these youth in the group if the physical well-being of the other group members and staff can be safeguarded.

(5) The Large Group should not be conducted for more than 90 minutes at a time. Every 90 minutes, the group members should be given a 15-minute break. This allows youth to go to the restroom and get water. During the break, staff may use the time by:
- Convening a brief staff planning session
- Meeting with positive youth and reviewing expectations for positive behavior
- Meeting with oppositional youth one-on-one and confronting them
- Calling the parents of oppositional youth and conducting a telephone conference

Large Group is conducted until the goal is attained or until staff are sure that the threat of physical danger has passed. It is important to be flexible. Sometimes the goal set by staff prior to the group cannot be met. Still, it may be possible to attain some other goal that ensures the physical well-being of youth and staff. Regardless of the actual goal attained, consequences should be given to the youth who were the cause of the problem that necessitated the Large Group. If the youth were cooperative and readily accepted responsibility for their problems, this should soften the consequences. Furthermore, youth who are disruptive during Large Group should be given consequences, e.g., restriction of free time, community service activity, or restriction of commissary privileges.

DAILY GROUPS

Whereas Called Groups are designed to have a positive effect on the milieu, the Daily Group is intended to have a positive effect on the individual. Because the two types of groups differ in terms of their goals, they also differ in terms of format. Perhaps the most significant difference between the two types of groups can be reduced to a single issue. In a Daily Group, the youth is asked why he behaves as he does, but the why question is actively avoided in Called Groups. The question "Why?" requires a youth to explore and explain his motives and goals. This is the goal of the Daily Group and the basis of long-term change within the individual.

Although the delinquent's motives and goals are constant issues in Daily Group, three specific techniques are used to help the youths understand and change their motives, goals and behavior: Offense Cycle, Victim Empathy, and Recidivism Prevention. Each of these concepts will be discussed fully later in this chapter.

Every well conducted Daily Group is comprised of four distinct components: the self-report, assigning the focus for the group, problem solving, and the conclusion. A description of each component will be provided. This description will include practical guidelines for the group counselor.

Daily Group Components

Self-Report. Each youth gives an accounting of his/her personal behavior since the last session. The self-report focuses primarily on problems, but youth can also report on successes. Youth also report on any assignments the counselor has given. The group counselor should not rely on youth to accurately report on themselves; delinquents tend to omit facts that they deem unpleasant. Thus, the group counselor must read the facility log and check with other staff prior to the session to know if a youth is omitting information. When possible, written documentation of problems should be brought to the session. This can help the counselor confront the youth about omissions or distortions. The following are the guidelines for the Self-Report:

(1) Each youth takes a turn and reports on problem behaviors or significant successes since the last session. A youth offers no explanations of problem behaviors. A Self-Report is objective and matter-of-fact. A youth must also report on the status of any assignments given by the counselor, e.g., offense cycle worksheet (see Appendix A).

(2) Group members listen to the report. If the youth omits a problem(s), the group members raise their hands and wait to be called on by the youth giving the Self-Report. When called upon, the youth's peers describe the omitted problem(s).

(3) If the youth fails to report problems that the group counselor is aware of, the group counselor reminds the youth of the omitted problem(s).

(4) If youth use problem labels, e.g., "power problem," to aid Self-Reports, it is not acceptable for a youth to simply report the problem label, "I had a power problem." If a youth makes a statement using the problem label, he must also

describe the problem, e.g., "I had a power problem, I purposely set up Neil for detention because I wanted to get back at him." Youths who fail to describe the problem and simply hide behind jargon must be confronted by the other group members, e.g., "Express your problem."

(5) Inevitably, problems do occur in the Self-Report. It is a good way for the group counselor to assess the group members' honesty and ability to work. Typical problems include:

- A youth tries to take up too much time by over reporting.
- A problem-solving session may occur as a youth reports problems.
- Too much time is spent in Self-Report (this may be rigged or the group may actually require more training on how to make Self-Reports).
- A youth may report no problems, but everyone knows that the youth has had problems.
- The group members do not bring up problems of a youth who says he has no problems.
- A youth minimizes a problem.
- A youth exaggerates a problem.
- A youth projects the blame for a problem.
- A youth is vague in reporting a problem.

The Self-Report is a good way to ensure that each group member says something in each group. It should be noted that problem reporting is an unnatural act for the delinquent who tries to appear flawless. Still, it is important to develop the skill of positive self-criticism and overcome the tendency to front.

During a group session, it may be necessary for the group counselor to give the Self-Report for one or more youths in the group. This may be necessary if a youth is too new or too negative to provide an accurate self-report. Ideally, the youths should give their own Self-Report. Only in rare instances should the counselor take on this responsibility. The counselor who does take on the responsibility of reporting on youth should develop a plan whereby the youth will eventually begin doing their own Self-Report.

Assigning the Focus of Group. Based on the Self-Reports, the focus of the group session is determined. During a single group session there may be more than one focus. However, it is important to not focus on too many different issues during a group session. Trying to handle more than two issues in a group may result in superficial problem solving; therefore, two issues is the maximum number of problems that should be addressed in a session. If more issues are handled, one needs to determine who is being superficial: the group members or the group counselor.

Either the group counselor or the group members can assign the focus of the meeting. The counselor should assign the focus of the group meeting when there is an important issue that the group counselor wants to address, or the group is comprised of new or negative members who may not address the appropriate issue(s).

Ideally, the group members should be the ones to assign the focus. This helps the group counselor to avoid being perceived as picking on a particular youth. The group counselor allows each member in the group to say who should be the focus of group. After the group members have had their say, the group can vote to determine who should receive the focus of the group. Sometimes several votes may be taken. Members may be given the opportunity to explain their votes. The group counselor can resolve indecision by assigning a focus. However, it may be more instructive for the counselor to watch how the group assigns the focus, e.g., "Is one youth working hard to get the focus? If so, why? Does he want to use the group time constructively? Is he a scapegoat? Is someone manipulating him?" These and other questions may be answered by careful observation on the part of the counselor. The answers to these questions can often provide the counselor with an indication of how well the group is functioning.

There are criteria that should be used when assigning the focus for the group to ensure that the appropriate youth receives the focus. To the extent possible, the group members should use these criteria to assign the focus. The group counselor should also teach the youth priorities of these criteria for assigning the focus. The following is a rank order listing of the criteria for assigning the focus of a group:

(1) A threat of harm to peers or staff, threat of escape, or recent physical aggression is present.
(2) A youth is ready to present the offense cycle, victim empathy, or recidivism prevention worksheets or other assignments.
(3) Discharge or release is impending.
(4) A youth needs the other group members to help solve a problem.

Problem Solving. The individual who is the focus of the group session must try to understand and resolve a problem. Ultimately, the youth must plan and use appropriate behaviors, which can replace the identified problem behavior. Although there are many different types of problem-solving processes, most of the successful problem-solving processes share certain common elements. The steps of the problem-solving process used in this group counseling approach are listed below:

(1) *Identification of the problem.* This entails describing who, what, when, where and how of a recent problem experienced by the youth. The group members must take the role of detectives. They must pin down the specifics of the problem. The group counselor guides the discussion to ensure that all the facts are uncovered. At this point in the problem-solving process, the focus is upon the current problem. No attempt is made to relate the problem to the past or the future. There is a definite here-and-now emphasis.

(2) *Acceptance of the problem.* The youth being confronted with the problem must accept ownership of the problem. That is, the youth must admit that he engaged in the problem behavior as described by the group. This step in the process is crucial. A youth must admit to having a problem prior to developing solutions for the problem. A youth may try to defeat this step in the process by minimizing the problem or superficially accepting the problem. Such behavior needs to be confronted and eliminated by the group members.

(3) *Explanation of why the behavior is a problem.* Once a problem has been identified and the youth has accepted responsibility for it, the youth must identify why the behavior is a problem. The context for explaining why the behavior is a problem is twofold. First, the youth must explain how prosocial values and norms were violated by the behavior. In essence, this is an opportunity for a youth to begin developing a sense of values and morals. Second, the youth must identify the delinquent characteristics which were the basis of the problem behavior. This provides the youth with an opportunity to begin to see the connection between delinquent characteristics and problem behavior. It is important to analyze the behavior from both the context of social norms and delinquent characteristics.

(4) *Connecting the problem to similar problems.* The youth assesses the problem being addressed and determines if it is part of a pattern. It is at this time that the motives and goals underlying the behavior are explored. The youth must be helped to determine why the behavior is occurring and develop an understanding of the role played by the delinquent characteristics. The group members must help the youth identify the past, present and possible future manifestations of the delinquent characteristics. If a youth has presented his offense cycle worksheet or recidivism prevention worksheet in group, this material should be used to understand his current problem (see Cognitive Intervention). If the youth has not presented these worksheets, then the discussion should help prepare him to do so.

(5) *Developing alternatives.* The youth must develop an alternative way of behaving based upon prosocial norms and attitudes. That is, the youth must plan to use behaviors that can replace the problem behavior. The group members help the youth by making suggestions. Group members should confront the youth when the planned behavior is inadequate or inappropriate. Ultimately, the youth must come up with his/her own plan for behavior. Although group members offer advice and suggestions, their main job is that

of providing feedback to the youth. As necessary, the group members also provide support for the youth.

(6) *Follow-up.* No plan for change is complete without a follow-up plan. There are many ways to follow up on a plan, e.g., have staff or peers monitor the youth or have the youth make a report in a future group session. Any follow-up procedure is adequate. It is important to specify how follow-up will occur.

Conclusion. The conclusion of the meeting is an important determinant of the effectiveness of the session. A good conclusion reinforces the changes a youth is trying to make. Two basic activities occur during the conclusion. First, a summary of the meeting is offered. Either the group counselor or a group member can summarize the meeting. Unless there is a compelling reason for the group counselor to summarize, e.g., too many new members, a group member should summarize. The other activity that occurs during the conclusion is the counselor teaching and reinforcing. The group counselor concludes by reinforcing positive interactions and labeling and devaluing negative interactions. The group counselor, in essence, teaches positive values and helps youth distinguish delinquent and nondelinquent values. Overall, the conclusion of group is powerful and should be used to shape behavior beyond the group session. In order to have a powerful conclusion, there are specific things that a group counselor can and should do:

(1) Confront negative, delinquent behavior in an open honest way
(2) Interpret the underlying goals and motives of youth
(3) Identify patterns of negative behavior and connect such patterns with present and past problems
(4) Reinforce appropriate use of the concepts of offense cycle, victim empathy, and recidivism prevention

The group counselor must recognize the conclusion of group as a powerful therapeutic tool. The effective group counselor will be thinking about the conclusion throughout group and making decisions about what will be reinforced and what will be confronted.

SEED GROUPS

In order to conduct group counseling, there first must be a group. Good groups do not just spring to life. Forming a group requires a great deal of work. The first step in forming a group is pregroup training, i.e., training group members how to use group counseling. A pregroup training curriculum is presented in another chapter. This material should be used as part of orientation for new youth. Ideally, new youth should be maintained in an orientation group until they have mastered the group skills. But the use of pretraining and orientation is insufficient when the task at hand is creating a facilitywide group program.

Sometimes a group program must be implemented throughout an entire facility. The technique used in this situation is called the Seed Group Technique. This technique entails training a select few youth to use group. These youth are then dispersed to other groups throughout the facility and they assist group counselors in developing these groups. Thus, they are dispersed like seeds in hopes of harvesting positive groups. The following are guidelines for developing Seed Groups:

Step One

The group counselor determines how many youth will be involved in the Seed Group at any point in time. The number of youth involved in the Seed Groups depends upon the size of the facility. In facilities of 25 or less, only seven or eight youth need to be involved. In large campuses with many dorms, it may be wise to consider implementing the Seed Group in one or two dorms at a time. This way staff can learn from the group counselor's mistakes and successes.

Step Two

The group counselor identifies the positive peer leaders in a cottage. This entails setting behavioral criteria for what constitutes a positive leader, e.g., influences peers, prevents or stops negative acting-out and is able to verbalize thoughts and feelings. The youth who appear to meet the criteria are contacted and the counselor lets them know they have been selected as members of a Seed Group. It is explained to them that this is an honor. The group counselor gets them excited and interested.

Step Three

Didactic training is conducted using the pregroup training curriculum contained in this book. Each training issue should be thoroughly covered and it should be ensured that all youth are properly trained.

Step Four

The group is conducted for a two-week period. The counselor continues to be didactic. As group members begin to show they can function appropriately, more autonomy is given to them. The counselor continues to remind them that their goal is to become group experts. They will ultimately teach and model for their peers. The counselor sets the expectation that the Seed Group members must model appropriate behavior throughout the day.

Step Five

While facilitating in the Seed Group, the counselor begins pregroup training for other youth. As with the Seed Group, it is ensured that all youth are thoroughly trained. The counselor explains to them that they will be joined shortly by peers who are specially trained to be positive group members.

Step Six

After the Seed Group has demonstrated proficiency, it is dispersed. This entails taking members from the Seed Group and members in the pregroup training and forming new groups. The group counselor carefully considers how to match Seed Group members with other members. For example, he or she is sure to match Seed Group members with peers on level of intelligence, level of sophistication, ability to lead, and other relevant variables. He or she definitely avoids assigning Seed Group members to groups in which they could be abused or discounted. The Seed Group members must be viewed as leaders in their groups.

Step Seven

The group leader assumes a directive role initially. As the group begins to show cohesiveness, more responsibility can be given to the group. The group counselor uses Seed Group members extensively in the beginning. Whenever possible, the counselor allows the Seed Group members to conduct group.

Step Eight

New members are admitted to the group after they have completed training. Each facility should have a mechanism in place which ensures that new youth receive appropriate training. Ideally this should be an orientation program conducted by specific staff.

Once the groups have been established, they begin to take on a life of their own. That is, groups develop and evolve at their own rate. Some groups, however, do not evolve. They seem to stagnate. It is important for the group counselor to be aware of the different levels of development of the group. His or her response should be varied according to the group's level of development. Consider Table 3.1 that depicts the group developmental level and the counselor's role (Yalom, 1975).

TABLE 3.1   Group Development Issues and the Counselor's Role

Level of Development	Issue	Counselor's Role
New group just being formed or an old group in which there is little trust	In or Out—Group members are sizing up the members and the counselor in an attempt to determine if they want in or out of the group.	The members are taught group skill. The counselor sets values and expectations, model values and desired behaviors.
Group members are familiar but not supportive	Top or Bottom—Members are vying for power in the pecking order. They are trying to determine if they are at the top or the bottom of the pecking order. Attacks on the group counselor are not uncommon.	The counselor confronts and sets limits on negative behavior. Reinforcement of positive behavior continues. Sessions are structured so that positive youth receive more power and attention.
Group members are positive and supportive.	Near or Far—The group is cohesive and positive. The issue is how near (intimate) they are willing to be. The group is powerful and therapeutic.	The counselor is supportive. The group is allowed to progress at its own rate. Limit-setting is rare. The counselor can enjoy group.

Groups not only evolve, they regress. The addition of a new group member can send a group into a regressive tailspin. The group counselor who can diagnose the group's level of development and respond appropriately will be the effective group counselor.

COGNITIVE INTERVENTIONS

A youth who is participating in this group program must expend a great deal of energy and undergo much stress in an effort to change. The counselor should do all that he or she can to ensure that these changes are permanent. The research shows that cognitive behavior interventions tend to have the greatest impact on a youth's long-term adjustment (Gendreau & Ross, 1984; Garrett, 1985; Gendreau & Ross, 1987). Furthermore, it is suggested that the interventions be specific to the problem (Beutler, 1979). Consequently, the limit and lead program emphasizes three issues that youth must address during the time that they are group participants. The issues and time frames for addressing these issues are:

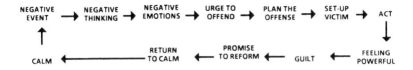

Figure 3.1. Offense Cycle

Offense Cycle—within 60 days of admission to the program
Victim Empathy—within 90 days of admission to the program
Recidivism Prevention—at least 30 days prior to discharge

These time frames are based upon a program that is four to six months in duration. Naturally, the time frames can be altered to reflect the average length of stay for a particular facility. The requirements for addressing these issues follow.

Offense Cycle

Offenses do not just happen. There are events that trigger very specific thoughts and feelings which result in the delinquent planning and executing an offense (Ryan et al., 1987). Although the events triggering this process vary from person to person, each offender actually has a specific and identifiable pattern of committing an offense. This specific pattern is called the *offense cycle.*

The notion of the offense cycle is not new. Indeed, it is preceded by at least two similar concepts found in two very different schools of psychology. First is the concept of the neurotic paradox as described in the psychoanalytic approach. The neurotic paradox is a maladaptive behavior pattern which a person exhibits in response to anxiety. It is maladaptive in that it interferes with social functioning and it does nothing to address the source of the stress. This is the essence of the offense cycle: *It detracts from social adaptation and it causes more problems than it solves.* Second is the concept of habit as explained by the behaviorists. A habit is a routine but complex behavior pattern engaged in by an individual to respond to specific stimuli that act as triggers for this behavior pattern. Although offense cycles are not habits, the conceptualization of offenses as a complex behavioral routine makes it similar to the behaviorist's concept of habit.

Regardless of one's theoretical orientation, the offense cycle provides a good framework within which the delinquent can begin to understand and change his or her behavior. In order to use the concept of the offense cycle, the offender is presented with a generic offense cycle. Then he or she is asked to personalize it and discover his or her own offense cycle. The generic offense cycle can be described as in Figure 3.1.

In order to personalize the offense, the youth must identify how he or she enacts each step in the offense cycle. Definitions for each step in the cycle are:

- *Negative event.* This is the trigger for the offense cycle. It may be one cata-strophic negative event or it may be a minor negative event occurring in the context of a chain of negative events. The negative events most likely to trigger the offense cycle are interpersonal conflict and events causing lower self-esteem.

- *Negative thinking.* The youth begins to have negative thoughts about the trigger event. The most common thoughts include, It is not fair, I cannot stand it, or I deserve better. It is quite common to find thinking that corresponds to the delinquent characteristics discussed previously.

- *Negative emotions.* As a result of the negative thinking, negative emotions begin to arise. The negative emotions are uncomfortable and unpleasant. Due to this discomfort, a fight or flight response is mobilized.

- *Urge to offend.* The delinquent's first relief from the stress of the negative event is the urge to offend. The urge is a combination of a fantasy and feeling. The fantasy about the offense distracts the youth from thinking about the negative trigger event. This causes some relief from the distress. But there is more. As the youth fantasizes about the offense, he begins to feel better. Perhaps the offense entails dominating others. Or perhaps the fantasy is one of vengeance. The exact content of the fantasy is not as crucial as the function it serves: It relieves the delinquent of stress and creates a sense of wellbeing.

- *Plan the offense.* The amount of planning is variable. Some offenses occur impulsively and are based largely upon the urge to offend; however, some offenses are carefully planned. From a psychological perspective, it must be recognized that planning an offense can be very exciting and, consequently, self-reinforcing.

- *Set-up the victim.* Offenses against people are the most obvious offenses in which the set-up is a factor. Other offenses such as burglary or auto theft may not entail an elaborate plan to set-up the victim. In some offenses, there may seem like there is no set-up, e.g., victimless crimes. Every offense, however, should be scrutinized on this issue. Careful scrutiny may reveal that there was a set-up. Consider the so-called victimless crime of prostitution. It is argued that there is no victim since both parties were mutually consenting. The role of the prostitute, however, is actually to set-up the client. The prostitute must dress and act seductively and be at the right place at the right time to be successful. Hence, there is a set-up. Viewed in a similar manner, drug sales also have a set-up component. The issue of victim set-up deserves careful consideration in each offense cycle.

- *Act.* Acting-out the planned offense. Issues such as the use of force and sadistic or bizarre characteristics of the offense merit attention.
- *Feeling powerful.* During and immediately after the offense, the delinquent feels excited and electrified. This is a very desirable state for the delinquent. It tends to cancel out the negative feelings caused by the negative trigger event.
- *Guilt.* It is not uncommon for the delinquent to feel guilt after an offense. The guilt usually arises from the awareness that other people do not act this way.
- *Promise to reform.* The delinquent has many ways of handling guilt. Minimization and projection are typical techniques for guilt evasion. In the offense cycle, guilt is evaded by making the promise to never act that way again. The delinquent believes the promise. The delinquent feels secure and confident that he or she can remain committed to his or her promise. Based upon this reliance on the promise, the delinquent returns to a state of calm. Since the delinquent has made no real personal changes, however, it is only a matter of time before another negative event triggers the offense cycle. The offense process is triggered and the cycle repeats itself, time and time again.

In an effort to help youth begin to identify and control their own offense cycles, the Offense Cycle Worksheet was devised (Appendix A). The Offense Cycle Worksheet is designed to analyze one offense in detail. The youth concentrates on one offense and answers the questions on the worksheet. The answers to the questions provide the youth with an awareness of how the offense cycle was enacted for that specific offense. Sometimes it is very difficult to uncover one's offense cycle by completing one Offense Cycle Worksheet. In fact, it is best if several Offense Cycle Worksheets are completed, each focusing upon a different offense. Then, the answers found on the Offense Cycle Worksheets can be transcribed to the Offense Cycle Summary Worksheet (Appendix A). Summarizing the answers of several Offense Cycle Worksheets on the Summary Worksheet allows patterns to emerge. The combined information of several Offense Cycle Worksheets makes it easier to identify the type of negative events, thoughts, and feelings that trigger the offense cycle. It is also easier to detect the maladaptive ways in which negative events are handled.

The youth must complete the Offense Cycle Worksheet outside of group. The youth's peers or counselor assist in completing the worksheet. After completing the worksheet, it is presented in a Daily Group session. Each youth must present his offense cycle within 60 days of admission to the program.

After the youth completes his Offense Cycle Worksheet, it is not simply forgotten. The youth who truly personalizes the offense cycle can use the information to understand new problems as they arise. The new problems do not have to be formal offenses. Rather, they can be any transgression, large or small, that violates a social norm or exploits another person. For example, the offense cycle can be used by a youth to understand such behavior as manipulating a weak peer, cheating on a test, or not performing assigned tasks. These violations are not formal offenses but they are behaviors that the youth should recognize as negative and should attempt to eliminate.

Victim Empathy

Most delinquents would not behave as they do if they had empathy for their victims. Indeed, lack of empathy is a crucial factor in maintaining a delinquent life-style (Samenow, 1984). Thus it is important that delinquents develop empathy in hopes that it may prevent future delinquent acts. This emphasis upon victim empathy occurs in the context of a growing sentiment among criminal justice professionals that crime victims deserve our support and attention (Davis, 1987). Most professionals have begun to realize that crime victims have been ignored and even suffered the additional indignity of seeing an enormous investment by society in those who commit crimes and virtually none for the victims (Bard & Sangrey, 1984). Therefore this group program places specific emphasis upon the issue of victim empathy.

Victim empathy must be developed experientially. That is, the youth must have an emotional experience or, more properly, an emotional awakening if victim empathy is to be developed. Several different structured experiences can be used to help develop victim empathy. Some of the more popular interventions currently used to develop victim empathy are listed here:

- *Offense reenactment.* The offender is required to do a role play of his committing offense. A synopsis of the committing offense is prepared by the offender and is used as a script. Other members of the group may play parts in the role play. Mannequins may also be used if the offense is an offense against a person. After the role play is completed, the group discusses it with a focus on how the offender hurt the victim.

- *Victim letters.* These are letters that are never meant to be sent. The offender writes a letter to the victim apologizing and asking for forgiveness. The offender describes the emotional pain the victim experienced and expresses appropriate concern.

- *Victim groups.* A community group comprised of survivors of criminal acts meets with group members. The crime survivors describe how their lives have been affected by crime.

- *Family therapy.* The offender, a counselor, and the offender's family meet to discuss how the offense has affected the family. Emphasis is placed on how the family has had to alter its routine and how its relationship with neighbors and co-workers has been affected.

In this group program, empathy for victims is addressed through the use of the Victim Empathy Worksheet (Appendix A). The Victim Empathy Worksheet requires the youth to take a detailed look at how an offense has affected the victim and other people in the victim's life. In order to complete the Victim Empathy Worksheet, the youth must put him- or herself in the position of the victim. The youth must take stock of how the offense has affected the victim. For many youth, this may be the first time that they have stopped to consider how their behavior affects their victims. The goal of the Victim Empathy Worksheet is to create an awareness on the part of the youth that may make it more difficult for them to offend.

As with other worksheets assigned to the youth, the Victim Empathy Worksheet is completed outside the group session. The youth may receive help from staff or peers when completing the worksheet. The youth presents it during Daily Group counseling session. Other group members listen to the presentation and confront the youth for failures to exhibit a depth of understanding of the empathy issue. He or she is also rewarded or praised for appropriate awarenesses and disclosures regarding empathy.

In a program that has an average length of stay of 6 months, the Victim Empathy Worksheet should be completed between 60 and 90 days into the youth's tenure. The time frame for completing the worksheet can be adjusted according to the youth's length of stay. While there is flexibility in the timing of this worksheet, there is no flexibility in the sequencing of this worksheet. The Victim Empathy Worksheet is always done subsequent to the Offense Cycle Worksheet. The Offense Cycle Worksheet established that the youth is responsible for the offense and other delinquent actions. The Victim Empathy Worksheet attempts to help the youth develop some feelings about being responsible.

Recidivism Prevention

There is a growing awareness that offenders must be taught how to maintain the therapeutic progress that they have attained. Preparing offenders for the challenges of life after the program is a common way to help them maintain therapeutic gains. This preparation begins while the offender is still in treatment and is designed to keep the offender from relapsing into the offense cycle (Pithers et al., 1983). Thus the training is called *recidivism prevention.*

Recidivism is conceptualized as a process similar to the offense cycle (Gorski & Miller, 1979). Offenders are taught that recidivism does not just happen. Instead, the offender makes decisions and behaves in such a manner that recidivism is inevitable. Offenders are presented with a generic recidi-

Figure 3.2. Recidivism Process

vism model (Marlatt & Gordon, 1987) and work to identify and prevent their own recidivism process. The generic recidivism model is shown in Figure 3.2.

For each step in the recidivism process, the offender identifies the personal ways it may manifest. Having identified a potential behavior that could lead to recidivism, the youth plans ways to avoid that behavior and stop the recidivism process. The following describes each step in the recidivism process:

(1) *Dangerous decisions.* Any decision that puts the youth in a situation conducive to crime. It may be a decision to associate with certain people or to live or work in high-risk situations. Often the youth fails to recognize the dangerousness of these decisions.

(2) *High-risk situations.* Situations conducive to recidivism, e.g., being alone with money, or any situation in which criminal activity is not easily detected.

(3) *Lapses.* A lapse is defined as a fantasy or an urge to reoffend. Recall that the urge to offend is a mental activity. It is comprised of a fantasy and a feeling regarding the commission of an offense.

(4) *Low self-esteem.* The mental lapse often triggers negative thoughts about self, e.g., "I guess I am no good. I am thinking about reoffending. Why even try to stop myself?" The low self-esteem seems to clear the way for the youth to fall back into the offense cycle.

The Recidivism Prevention Worksheet is designed to help youth recognize their own personal recidivism process. This worksheet should be completed outside the group session. When it is completed, it should be presented during a Daily Group. The counselor or the youth's peers may assist in completing the worksheet. The worksheet should be completed at least 30 days prior to the youth leaving the program. When possible, the youth should complete the worksheet even earlier. This allows for more processing of recidivism issues. Two recidivism worksheets have been devised. Worksheet I should be completed by all youth. Worksheet II should be completed as time allows.

Recidivism is a process that unfolds over time. Until a youth has been prepared to combat recidivism, we cannot be sure we have done everything we can to help that youth. Each youth should be taught that recidivism begins within the person and is most likely to occur as a result of personal problems. Youth must be taught to recognize this process and overcome it.

SPECIAL COUNSELING SERVICES

Called Groups and Daily Groups are designed to help youth eliminate delinquent behaviors and begin meeting their needs by using positive, prosocial behavior. In the course of treating the many youth who have been adjudicated delinquent, it has become apparent that not all these youth can have their needs adequately met by the basic counseling program. These youth are "special needs" youth. For these youth, special counseling services are provided.

Two types of specialized counseling services can be offered. First there are specialized programs. Specialized programs are self-contained programs, e.g., a halfway house or a dorm in an institution. A specific type of youth is placed in the program making the population homogeneous. Staff members are trained to respond to the uniqueness and the nuances of the special population. The counseling program is modified to impact the unique deficits and problems of the youth in the program. In general, these programs are only used when the force of the milieu is required to impact the problems, e.g., substance abusers or sex offenders. Second there are specialized groups. Special groups are offered once or twice a week to specific youth. Youth living in the general population attend these groups. Group membership is determined by the presence or absence of a specified problem, e.g., low self-esteem or previous sexual victimization. Staff who conduct the groups receive special training in that area. Groups are usually close-ended and are only 6 to 10 weeks in duration.

In juvenile corrections today, a finite number of special programs and services has been developed. The most ubiquitous services currently offered are for aggressive youth, sex offenders, and substance abusers (Gendreau & Ross, 1987). Although a limited number of specialized services are currently offered, the potential variety of special services is limitless. In fact, if a problem can be well defined, a special counseling program could probably be developed. Whether or not a special counseling program is developed depends upon a number of clinical and administrative factors. The following procedure can be followed to assess the clinical and administrative issues relevant to such a decision. The procedure is comprised of two phases. Phase One is the needs assessment, which provides the information necessary to determine if a special service is warranted. Phase Two is used to plan and implement a special program.

Phase One: Needs Assessment

A needs assessment is conducted to determine if a special service is warranted. The decision to implement a special service is based upon two needs: clinical and administrative.

When addressing the clinical need for the special service, the focus is upon the ability to treat the problem using the basic group program. Consideration is also given to the prognosis for those who may need, but do not receive, the special services.

When addressing the administrative need for the special service, attention is focused on the agency's obligation to provide such a service and the community's expectation that such a service be rendered. Consideration is also given to staff and fiscal resources. Guidelines for conducting a needs assessment are:

(1) *Problem definition.* The first task is to operationally define the problem for which the special service will be offered. The problem must be defined in terms of quantifiable or observable criteria so the prevalence of the problem can be determined. For example, if offering a group counseling program for low self-esteem youth is under consideration, low self-esteem could be operationally defined as a score on a psychological test that measures self-esteem. Objective criteria are the basis for deciding if a youth does or does not possess the problem.

(2) *Survey.* Using the operational definition of the problem, a survey is conducted. The survey can target all youth residing in the agency at a particular point in time, or the survey can be a sample of youth admitted to the agency during a specified time period. Either method is acceptable in determining the scope of a problem. Regardless of the survey method used, it is important that those conducting the survey be trained to use the survey questions and criteria in a consistent manner. High interrater reliability is essential to produce usable results.

(3) *Treatability.* This issue pertains to how well the youth are being served by the basic group program. Several questions are posed to direct care and professional staff.

   • Does a youth with this type of problem respond well to the basic group program?
   • Does a youth with this type of problem seem less prepared for the community at the time of release?
   • Does it seem that more could be done for this type of youth?
   • Do youth with this type of problem recidivate more often than those without this type of problem?

The fourth question can and should be asked of staff. Their anecdotal and clinical impressions are valuable. However, agencies with sophisticated information systems can also address this question with a study of recidivism data.

(4) *Resource analysis.* Administrative staff must provide input on the availability of staff time and physical space to conduct a program. The resource analysis should be considered from two perspectives:
- What resources are needed to implement a special program?
- What resources are currently available to implement this special program?

(5) *Impact analysis.* The impact analysis addresses the issue of the results of not implementing a special service for youth with the identified problem. The focus of the analysis is concerned with how no program would impact the youth's post-release adjustment, the safety of the community, and the prevailing political and societal attitudes at that point in time.

Using the guidelines provided above, a needs assessment can be conducted that will provide sufficient information to determine if a special counseling service should be implemented. The decision to implement a service should be based upon the feasibility of the program. Programs are considered feasible and necessary if there exists a sizable number of youth who cannot get their needs met through the basic group program, and if failure to meet these needs would result in negative effects for the youth, the community, and possibly the agency.

Phase Two: Program Design

Assuming that the results of the needs assessment indicate that a special counseling service is warranted, a proposal must be developed to deliver the needed services. The proposal must specify how the special needs will be met and what resources will be allocated to this effort. A program proposal format is provided as a guideline for designing special counseling services. Use of these guidelines ensures that the factors relevant to program design and implementation are analyzed prior to the initiation of the special counseling services.

SPECIAL SERVICES PROPOSAL

Introduction

A brief narrative is presented describing the problem addressed by the special service. The narrative defines the problem and explains why it is a special problem. A brief description of the special service is also offered, indicating whether the special service is a program or a group. A rationale for the use of the selected intervention is presented.

Literature Review

The literature review is a brief synopsis of selected books and articles pertaining to the special problem. An attempt is made to identify research or clinical literature that provide the conceptual foundation of the program. The review of the literature should enable one to use existing information and avoid reinventing the wheel.

Intake Procedures

Intake procedures that will ensure evaluation of all youth for program eligibility need to be specified. The intake procedures should be based upon eligibility and disqualification criteria. Eligibility criteria should be observable traits or behaviors. For example, if the special group is for aggressive youth, then the eligibility criteria could be the frequency of aggressive acts in a specified period or a score on an objective psychological test designed to measure aggression. Disqualification criteria should exclude youth from the program who would not be appropriate. For example, a youth may meet the eligibility criteria for an aggression control group, but the youth may also be psychotic. The psychosis would prevent the youth from benefiting from the treatment. Hence, psychosis would be the disqualification criteria.

A detailed intake process based upon these criteria should also specify the staff responsible for screening youth and the staff responsible for assigning youth to the program. It is useful if the staff conducting the screening are different from the staff making the program assignment. This provides for a review mechanism within the intake process.

Treatment Procedures

The type of intervention to be used is described. The responsibilities and duties of the program staff are delineated. It is also useful to describe the phases of treatment for the youth. Most special programs should be time limited. Within the specified time frames, the treatment sequence could be specified as follows: (a) *beginning*—describe how rapport will be established and how denial and defensiveness will be eliminated; (b) *middle*—describe the issues to be addressed, the interventions and techniques to be used and the expected client behavior/defenses; (c) *ending*—describe how the youth will use new awareness to change behavior, describe attempts to generalize change from the treatment setting to other settings.

Program Evaluation

Two types of program evaluation measures are possible: longitudinal studies and clinical outcome. If a longitudinal evaluation is used, it is necessary to conduct a follow-up over an extended period of time. A three-to five-year follow-up period is the minimum amount of time acceptable in a longitudinal study (Greer & Stuart, 1983). Negative measures such as recidivism and positive measures such as school attendance should be used (Andrews, 1983). The other method of program evaluation is the clinical outcome measure which requires pretesting and posttesting of youth using clinical questionnaires or psychological tests. This approach has the advantage of providing immediate results, but it cannot assess long-term behavioral change as is the case with the longitudinal approach. Regardless of which outcome evaluation method is employed, a control group should also be used.

Cost Analysis

The cost of running the program should be figured by accounting for the resources allotted to the program. Resources that need to be accounted for include staff, office space, supplies, and opportunity cost, i.e., what services or programs will suffer as a result of implementing the program. It is possible to go beyond simple cost analysis after the program has been implemented. It is recommended that a cost-benefit study also be conducted. Cost-benefit studies typically delineate the long term and sometimes hidden fiscal benefits of implementing a special program.

Program Implementation

A plan must be developed that describes how the staff will be trained and youth assigned to the program. It is likely that the program will need to be phased in. A time frame for phasing in the program should be provided. Other key issues that should be addressed include: developing administrative support, informing other staff about the program, and program monitoring.

The following outline for a special group for aggressive youth is presented here for the purpose of illustrating a completed proposal. Assume that the Phase I: Needs Assessment has been completed and there is a need for such a group. Consequently, a proposal for the group needs to be submitted. The following proposal outline is not fully elaborated. A fully elaborated proposal would be three to five pages. The following is merely an outline designed to demonstrate the proposal format.

TITLE AGGRESSION CONTROL SKILLS MODULE

Introduction

Youth at the facility have recently begun to exhibit increased aggressive behavior. During the last 6 months there has been a 15% increase in assaults by youth. Most of the assaults result from impulsiveness and poor frustration tolerance. Consequently, a cognitive behavioral group is proposed whereby youth could learn and practice self-control.

Literature Review

The contemporary literature suggests that aggressive youth must be taught self-control (Goldstein et al., 1986). The available research suggests that the social skills training approach is more effective than other approaches, e.g., nondirective (Kazdin et al., 1987).

Intake Procedure

Each youth assigned to the facility will be screened by a social worker. Screening is a two-step process. First, the youth's file is reviewed. An effort is made to determine if the youth has a history of violence, aggression or acting-out. Any youth with one or more documented incidents of aggressive behavior is referred for a screening interview. The screening interview comprises the second component of the intake process. During the interview, the social worker administers the Buss-Durke Hostility Scale (Buss & Durkee, 1957). Youth scoring above the cutoff score are deemed eligible for the group.

There are two instances when an otherwise eligible youth may be disqualified from the group: psychosis or mental retardation.

Treatment Procedure

There are three phases of treatment: (a) *beginning*—youth complete surveys and personal aggression history—the goal is to create self-awareness; (b) *middle*—youth learn a variety of self-control techniques, including relaxation training, cognitive rehearsal, and assertiveness training; and (c) *end*—youth practice self-control skills.

Program Evaluation

Two forms of evaluation will be used (a) group participants will receive pre- and posttesting, using the Buss-Durke Hostility Inventory; and (b) youth completing the group will be compared to similar youth who did not complete group on the number of assaults committed.

Cost Analysis

Existing equipment can be used, e.g., group room. Supplies will be purchased, e.g., paper and photocopy of workbooks. Approximately one and one-half hours of staff time will be consumed weekly. Forty-five minutes of clerical support will be used on a weekly basis. Limited opportunity costs will occur, i.e., no other component of the treatment program will be compromised. Cost-benefit projections suggest possible areas of savings in the following areas: destruction of state property, injury to staff, and disability payments.

Program Implementation

After the proposal is approved, the student workbook will be written. While the workbook is being written, staff will screen for group members. Prior to implementation, the group leader will conduct a 20-minute overview of the model at a facilitywide counselor meeting. After the group has commenced, the group leader will make weekly entries in the files of all youth in the group. A monthly report will be submitted to the facility administrator. The group will be time limited: 10 weeks. The group leader will obtain permission prior to initiating a second group.

Using this proposal format, it is possible to develop a detailed plan of the special service to be offered. The proposal should be reviewed by administrative and clinical staff to allow for the proposal to be debugged *prior* to implementation.

CHAPTER SUMMARY

In an effort to operationalize the concepts of the limit and lead group program, two treatment approaches were relied upon heavily. First, the traditional treatment approach of guided group interaction was utilized. This approach was selected because of its utility in creating and maintaining a safe, stable environment. Second, the treatment approach of cognitive behavioral therapy was used because the research indicates that this approach is effective in creating long-term changes. In combination, guided group interaction and cognitive behavioral therapy seem to provide the techniques for getting the attention of the juvenile delinquent, managing the milieu, and creating internal changes which will have a long-term effect on the behavior of those youth in the program.

Chapter 4

GROUP COUNSELOR TRAINING AGENDA AND CURRICULUM

The purpose of this chapter is to provide guidelines whereby group counselors may be trained to use the limit and lead group program. Although the target audience of this chapter is those who will be responsible for conducting training, several other audiences can benefit from it as well. Facility administrators can use this chapter to get a good idea of the resources (time and personnel) necessary for establishing a group counselor training program. Those aspiring to be group counselors will also find this chapter useful as it will give them an idea of the type of knowledge and experience necessary to become a group counselor.

Training guidelines are presented for two types of training: initial training and in-service training. Initial training is designed to introduce the limit and lead group program to those counselors with little knowledge and experience in dealing with juvenile delinquents. There is a strong didactic emphasis as it is assumed that trainees have no prior knowledge of this program. In-service training is provided to those who have completed the initial training. The in-service training is less didactic than the initial training and, like other forms of counselor education, the in-service training is based upon an apprenticeship model that emphasizes experiential learning.

In the guidelines for each type of training, several issues are addressed including learning objectives, training agendas and training exercises. Based upon the information and direction provided by these guidelines, it should be possible to implement and maintain a training program for the limit and lead group program.

INITIAL TRAINING

The initial training program is designed to introduce trainees to the concepts of the limit and lead group program and to let them practice the techniques described in this book. Given the inevitability of turnover in counselor staff, the initial training program should be conducted on a regular basis throughout the year. The exact frequency of scheduling the training depends upon the number of staff requiring training. The recommended ratio of trainers to trainees is 1:10. Training should take place when 10 to 15 staff require training. Because there are many group exercises on the agenda, the training requires four or more trainees. Scheduling more than 15 staff for training will create time and space problems, and will preempt experiential training.

LEARNING OBJECTIVES

Learning objectives are the specific goals to be obtained by the trainees. Since this is the first exposure trainees will have to the program, the objectives pertain largely to the person acquiring knowledge regarding the conceptual basis of the program and practicing the techniques described in Chapter 3.

Training objectives for the initial training

(1) Goals and philosophy
- To know that the group program is based upon several different types of groups
- To know the purpose of each type of group
- To know the goals for individuals in the program
- To know the goals for the group living environment
- To understand the philosophy of the group program

(2) Characteristics of delinquent youth
- To know the definition of delinquency
- To understand the continuum of delinquency
- To be able to recognize the five delinquent strengths as they occur in conversation and in the group setting
- To be able to recognize the five delinquent weaknesses as they occur in conversation and in the group setting
- To be able to recognize the nine delinquent defenses as they would appear in the counseling session

(3) Strength of adolescence
  - To be able to recognize and use the strengths when doing counseling

(4) Characteristics of group counselors
  - To know the characteristics of competent group counselors
  - To know how to behaviorally exhibit each of the characteristics
  - To know the two common mistakes of group counselors

(5) Interaction between the counselor and the youth
  - To be able to define the limit and lead strategy
  - To be able to list the five guidelines for setting limits, i.e., target behavior, set clear limits, set consistent limits, set firm limits, and set fair limits
  - To be able to list the three guidelines for leading, i.e., positive feedback, shaping, and prompt and fade
  - To know that the counselor's aim is to ultimately allow the youth to run the group
  - To know the 12 interventions and whether an intervention is designed to limit or lead
  - To be able to explain how a single intervention may be perceived differently by different youth
  - To be able to make interventions with an entire group

(6) Called group
  - To be able to identify the situations requiring a Huddle-up or Large Group
  - To be able to determine if it is appropriate to initiate a Huddle-up or Large Group
  - To be able to conduct a Huddle-up and Large Group
  - To know the four structural components of the Huddle-up and Large Group
  - To know when and how to delay the conclusion of a Called Group

(7) Daily group
  - To know the four distinct components of the Daily Group
  - To know the guidelines for self-reports
  - To know how to assign the focus of the group
  - To know the components of the problem-solving process
  - To know how to conclude the group
  - To know how to formulate and use a Seed Group

(8) Cognitive interventions
  - To be able to explain the offense cycle
  - To be able to use the Offense Cycle Worksheet and the Offense Cycle Summary Worksheet
  - To be able to explain the importance of victim empathy
  - To be able to use the Victim Empathy Worksheet

- To be able to explain the concept of recidivism
- To be able to use the Recidivism Prevention Worksheet

These learning objectives are based upon the information contained in the first three chapters of this book. If a trainee knows and understands the information presented in these chapters, the learning objectives would certainly be obtained. A trainee workbook is provided to assist with the learning process (Appendix A). To determine if a trainee has met the learning objectives, a posttraining test has been devised (Appendix B). This test should be administered to all those participating in the training program. A score of at least 80% should be obtained if a person is to be given credit for learning the information.

TRAINING AGENDA

The training agenda for the initial training is scheduled to be conducted over a 3-day period. The agenda is divided into six 4-hour segments. Each segment is designed to be responsive to the trainees' ability to learn at certain points of the day. Thus didactic material is typically presented during the initial segment of the morning training sessions. Experiential activities are scheduled as the first activity after lunch to circumvent problems that trainees have with being sleepy or distracted after their meal. Table 4.1 is the recommended training agenda to be followed for the initial training program.

It should be noted that within each 4-hour segment, an attempt is made to balance didactic and experiential training activities. Time should be allotted for questions and answers so that concepts and techniques may be integrated and any ambiguities may be cleared up. Breaking the training into 4 hour segments is also helpful to trainers. It allows them to pace themselves. The interplay of didactic experiential activities can also be used constructively by the trainer. During didactic activities, the trainer can set the tone and direction for the group program. Modeling of the group program goals and philosophy can also take place. During the experiential activities, the trainer can catch his breath as the trainees work in small groups. It also provides the trainer with an opportunity to assess each trainee's competence and comfort level with the material. Overall the training agenda is designed to afford an optimal experience to the trainers and trainees.

TRAINING EXERCISES

Training exercises are described for each training activity listed on the training agenda. The training exercises are described in such a manner that a trainer is given a clear idea about the goal, activity and procedures which

TABLE 4.1   Initial Training Agenda

Training Agenda		

DAY ONE

Module No.	Topic	Minutes
1	Overview of training	30
2	Definition of delinquency and characteristics of delinquent youth	105
Break		15
3	Limit and lead strategy	75
Lunch		60
4	Group simulation: Daily group	90
Break		15
5	Offense cycle	60
6	Group simulation: Huddle-up	75

DAY TWO

Module No.	Topic	Minutes
7	Counselor characteristics	60
8	Twelve interventions	90
Break		15
9	Victim empathy	60
Lunch		60
10	Group simulation: Daily Group	60
11	Recidivism prevention	60
Break		15
12	Group simulation: Large Group	90

DAY THREE

Module No.	Topic	Minutes
13	Group interventions	60
14	Delinquent defenses	60
Break		15
15	Group simulation: Daily Group	60
16	Limit and lead overview	45
Lunch		60
17	Group simulation: Large Group	90
Break		15
18	Group simulation: Huddle-up	90
19	Conclusion: Goals and philosophy	45

comprise a specific training exercise. While the description of the training exercises is detailed enough to structure the training experience, it does allow for some spontaneity and flexibility. Thus the training exercises should be thought of as the basis of the training and the trainer should depart from these exercises dependent upon the needs of the trainees and the expertise of the trainer. The Trainee Workbook is provided (Appendix A) to help structure the learning experience.

Module No. 1: Overview of training

Mode: Didactic

Goal: To provide trainees with an overview of the training agenda

Comments: Trainees are generally apprehensive on the first day of training. The trainer needs to put trainees at ease. This can be accomplished by:

• Informing the trainees what information they will be exposed to
• Setting a relaxed, comfortable tone for the training

Directions:

(1) State the title and purpose of the training.
(2) Ask trainees to complete the Personal Report in the Trainee Workbook. After completing the Personal Report, have trainees introduce themselves using the Personal Report as a guideline.
(3) Distribute the Training Agenda. Describe how the training is segmented into 4-hour training blocks. Point out that there are ample breaks and an opportunity for questions and answers.

Module No. 2: Definition of delinquency and characteristics of delinquent youth

Mode: Didactic

Goal: To teach trainees how much delinquents differ from other types of adolescent counseling patients

Comments: This exercise is usually well received by trainees who have a great deal of experience with delinquents. These trainees usually think that someone, i.e., the trainer, finally understands the delinquent. Trainees without much experience with delinquents usually find this presentation to be an eye-opener.

Directions:

(1) The material in Chapter 2 pertaining to delinquent characteristics is used as the training curriculum. The definition of delinquency and the continuum of delinquency are verbally presented. Then each delinquent characteristic is described and examples are given. Strengths of adolescence are also discussed.

(2) Trainees are allowed to use the material in the Trainee Workbook as a summary and outline of the presentation.

(3) As each characteristic is presented, trainees are asked to give examples. They usually have plenty.

(4) Trainees are asked to respond to the questions in the Trainee Workbook section titled *Distinguishing Different Types of Characteristics.* After completing this exercise, trainees compare and discuss the responses.

Module No. 3: Limit and lead strategy

Mode: Didactic

Goal: To teach trainees the concept of the limit and lead strategy used when counseling delinquents

Comments: The trainer has already introduced the trainees to the characteristics of delinquent youth. He/she points out that the counselor must limit delinquent strengths and lead delinquent weaknesses.

Directions:

(1) The trainer uses the material in Chapter 2 pertaining to the limit and lead strategy as the training curriculum. This material is presented to the trainees in a lecture format. The trainer must be sure to describe each item listed in the guidelines and give examples for each.

(2) The trainer presents the trainees with the scenarios in the Trainee Workbook. Some scenarios call for a limit response; some scenarios call for a lead response. Trainees are asked how they might respond in the various scenarios. Trainees must understand that different situations require different types of responses.

(3) The trainees are asked to present anecdotes in which they responded appropriately with a limit or a lead response. Critical feedback or support must be offered, depending upon the appropriateness of the behavior described in the anecdote.

Module No. 4: Daily Group

Mode: Experiential

Goal: To teach trainees how to conduct a Daily Group

Comments: Daily Groups are the core of the limit and lead group program. It is through the experiences and impact of the Daily Group that youth can make lasting changes. Consequently, trainees must learn this material well and be able to follow the format.

Directions:

(1) The trainer uses the text in Chapter 3 regarding Daily Groups as the basis of the training curriculum. The trainer begins with some introductory statements and provides an overview of the Daily Group. He or she must be sure to define each component of the Daily Group and explain why it is structured the way it is. Trainees use the section in the Trainee Workbook titled *Guidelines for Daily Groups* as an outline for the lecture.

(2) After each component of the Daily Group has been addressed, it is time to put them all together. The trainer role plays the counselor and five to six trainees volunteer to play group members. The role play should focus upon topics relevant to the delinquents. It is important to define the role that each trainee will play. For example, one trainee might portray a severe delinquent, another might play a mild delinquent, and so on. It is absolutely crucial that not every trainee role play a negative delinquent. This would undermine the role play. In fact, it is best if there is only one trainee role playing a negative youth. All other trainees should be positive.

(3) After the role play, the trainer elicits input from those involved in the role play. If the role play was videotaped, segments of the tape can be viewed and discussed.

(4) The trainer breaks the trainees into small groups of four or five persons. Trainees complete the Daily Group Worksheet. After the trainees complete this worksheet, they reconvene in the large group to discuss it.

Module No. 5: Offense cycle

Mode: Experiential

Goal: To teach the concept of the offense cycle, and to give trainees the experience of trying to change a personal habit

Comments: Trainees will be instructed to use the Offense Cycle Worksheet on a personal habit, e.g., smoking or overeating. The trainer ensures that trainees do not disclose too much, or talk about problems that are too personal. If the habit is too personal, then it might disrupt the cohesiveness of the trainees.

Directions:

(1) The trainer explains the concept of the offense cycle using the text in Chapter 3. Each step in the process is described. The trainer underscores that offenses do not just happen and that the delinquent is responsible for planning and enacting an offense.

(2) The trainer directs the trainees' attention to the Offense Cycle Worksheet. It is explained to them that this worksheet can be used with a variety of different bad habits, e.g., overeating or smoking cigarettes. The trainees are asked to select a personal bad habit that they would like to change. Trainees are cautioned not to select a problem that is too personal, e.g., marital problems. Then they are to complete the Offense Cycle Worksheet. On the items that refer to the offense, trainees should substitute their bad habit. Time should be allowed for trainees to complete the worksheet. The trainer circulates among the trainees and provides them with assistance.

(3) The trainer asks for trainees to volunteer to present their worksheets; fellow trainees critique them.

(4) After several worksheets have been presented, the trainer discusses the difficulty of talking about and changing bad habits. They are asked to empathize with the youth who will use the worksheet. Finally, trainees discuss possible problems youth may have when using the worksheet.

Module No. 6: Group simulation: Huddle-ups

Mode: Experiential

Goal: To teach trainees how and when to use the Huddle-up technique to maintain a safe and orderly facility environment

Comments: Trainees must come to realize that the Huddle-up technique is the group counselor's primary means of controlling the milieu. Trainees must learn not to overuse the technique so that it disrupts the daily schedule. Rather, they must learn to use it to maintain a safe and orderly facility environment.

Directions:

(1) The trainer uses the text in Chapter 3 pertaining to Huddle-ups as the basis of the training curriculum. Trainees may use the Guidelines for Huddle-ups as presented in the Trainee Workbook as an outline of the lecture.

(2) The text regarding *Recognizing the Need for a Huddle-up* and *Initiating a Huddle-up* can be presented in a didactic format.

(3) The text regarding *The Structure of a Huddle-up* should be presented in a didactic format. After lecturing on each of the four components of the Huddle-up, the Huddle-up is role played. As in previous training exercises, role playing begins with the trainer role modeling the counselor. The role play is allowed to occur for 5 to 10 minutes before being critiqued. Next, the trainees are divided into small groups of no more than five persons to role play the Huddle-up. The trainer ensures that as many trainees as possible have the opportunity to role play the counselor. Topics selected for role play should be similar to those that trainees will encounter when conducting a Huddle-up with a group of delinquents.

(4) The trainees are broken into small groups to complete the Huddle-up Worksheet from the Trainee Workbook. After completing the worksheet, all reconvene in the large group to discuss it.

Module No. 7: Counselor characteristics

Mode: Didactic

Goal: To teach trainees the specific counselor characteristics and corresponding behaviors that are prerequisites to effective counseling with juvenile delinquents

Comments: Trainees have been introduced to the characteristics of delinquents and the ways in which delinquents will resist counseling. Trainees have learned that the primary task of the counselor is to limit exploitive behavior and lead the youth towards prosocial behavior. The counselor characteristics should be presented in this context.

Directions:

(1) The text in Chapter 2 regarding Counselor Characteristics is used as the basis of this training exercise. The trainer refers to the description of counselor characteristics in the Trainee Workbook.

(2) Each of the counselor characteristics is presented with examples of behaviors representing each characteristic. Examples are solicited from trainees also.

(3) After all characteristics also have been presented, the trainees complete the Counselor Characteristics Worksheet. The worksheet is discussed after trainees complete it.

Module No. 8: Twelve interventions

Mode: Experiential

Goal: To introduce trainees to the counselor interventions and allow trainees to experience and practice how these interventions might be used

Comments: The trainer must use his time well. Didactic material must be presented and time must be allocated for role play.

Directions:

(1) The trainer uses the material in Chapter 2 pertaining to the 12 interventions as the basis of the training curriculum. He/she must be sure to present definitions and examples. Input and questions are requested during the presentation. Trainees may use the summary sheet in the Trainee Workbook to follow the presentation.

(2) After all the didactic material has been covered, five to six volunteers are solicited. The volunteers will role play group counseling members. The trainer will role play the group counselor. The trainer assigns roles to the trainees and ensures that no more than one or two trainees role play a negative, disruptive youth. A topic is selected and discussion begins. The trainer listens and intervenes frequently—perhaps more frequently than in a real counseling situation. The purpose of the frequent intervening is to demonstrate as many techniques as possible. The role play is allowed to go on for 10 minutes.

(3) After the role play, the group critiques it. Those involved as group members should describe how it felt when different interventions were made. Those observing the role play should offer input on how the interventions appeared to affect the group.

(4) After the discussion, the trainees should be broken into small groups of no more than five persons. Trainees complete the worksheet in the Trainee Workbook titled, *Using Intervention.*

(5) After each group has had an opportunity to complete the exercise, all return to the large group format. The trainees discuss the exercise with focus on the different impact that various interventions have made. Trainees are helped to begin developing a sense of timing, i.e., they receive feedback that will help them know when to limit and when to lead.

Module No. 9: Victim empathy

Mode: Experiential

Goal: To teach the concept of victim empathy and give trainees the experience of using the Victim Empathy Worksheet

Comments: Trainees will be asked to use the Victim Empathy Worksheet to analyze a personal situation. Not all items on the worksheet will be applicable to the trainees since the focus is upon delinquent behavior. Still, the trainees should be able to use the worksheet for a personal issue. The resistances trainees exhibit will be similar to the resistances exhibited by delinquent youth, and this should be pointed out.

Directions:

(1) The trainer discusses the concept of victim empathy using the text in Chapter 3 pertaining to victim empathy as the training curriculum.

(2) The trainer refers to the copy of the Victim Empathy Worksheet in the Trainee Workbook and explains each item on the worksheet.

(3) Trainees are instructed to complete the worksheet based upon a personal experience. Trainees must recall a situation in which they offended or disappointed another person. Based on the experience, trainees complete the worksheet. As trainees work on the worksheet the trainer circulates to ensure that trainees do not get bogged down.

(4) After the trainees complete the worksheets, the trainer asks for volunteers to present their worksheets. Those not making the presentation listen and offer a critique.

(5) After two or three trainees present their worksheets, the focus of discussion is shifted to: difficulties youth might have understanding the worksheet, and resistances and negative emotions that the worksheet might create.

Module Nos. 10 and 15: Group simulation: Daily Group

Mode: Experiential

Goal: To allow trainees to begin using their skill and knowledge to conduct a simulated group

Comments: Trainees must practice using the knowledge and skills they acquire in training. Many trainees will be embarrassed to role play a counselor. Still, it is essential that they practice in a safe setting before they go into a real life situation.

Directions:

(1) The trainer asks for six or seven people to volunteer for a group simulation.

(2) After the trainees have volunteered, someone is asked to volunteer to be a counselor. If the facility where the trainees work uses cotherapists, two trainees should volunteer.

(3) The trainer assigns roles to the other trainees. Again, limits are set on the number of people who role play disruptive delinquents.

(4) The trainer selects a topic and role playing begins. The role play is allowed to go on for about 20 minutes. About five minutes before the end of the role play, the counselor is directed to begin the concluding group.

(5) The trainer debriefs the group simulation. Those in the role play are asked about their experience. Trainees in the audience are asked for feedback.

(6) The process is repeated with a group of trainees who were not involved in the initial role play.

Module No. 11: Recidivism prevention

Mode: Experiential

Goal: To teach trainees how to use the Recidivism Prevention Worksheet

Comments: This is the third and final cognitive intervention to be used in the group. In addition to teaching trainees how to use this intervention, the trainees must also learn how to integrate the use of the cognitive worksheets in Daily Group.

Directions:

(1) The trainer uses the text in Chapter 3 pertaining to recidivism prevention as the basis of the training curriculum. The trainees are lectured on the concepts of recidivism and relapse. The trainer refers to the Recidivism Prevention Worksheet in the Trainee Workbook and defines each item on it.

(2) The trainer asks the trainees to complete the worksheet based upon a personal bad habit that they do not want to fall back into. The worksheets are discussed after the trainees complete them.

(3) The trainer explains to the trainees that youth must be trained to complete the three cognitive worksheets. This means that the counselor will have to meet with each youth individually and explain each worksheet. This requires three separate meetings to discuss each worksheet separately. The youth must complete their worksheets outside of group. After completing a worksheet, each youth must present it during a group session.

Module No. 12: Large Group

Mode: Experiential

Goal: To teach trainees how to use the Large Group technique to provide for a safe, secure facility environment

Comments: There are various types of large group meetings, e.g., student government or community meetings. The Large Group technique as presented in this group program is a dynamic problem-solving group. It is much more powerful than other less focused types of groups. Trainees should learn to recognize the force of this type of group and use it only when the situation warrants it.

Directions:

(1) The text in Chapter 3 pertaining to Large Groups is used as the basis for this training exercise.
(2) The trainer presents all of the material about the Large Group technique in a didactic format.
(3) After the lecture material has been presented, a Large Group is role played. This role play will take a little staging. First, several trainees will have to be selected to role play staff. Then, they should receive instructions as to the role they will play during the Large Group. Some trainees will sit in the group and verbally interact. Other trainees will walk around the outside of the group monitoring nonverbal cues and level of involvement. All other trainees will role play youth. Before beginning the role play, the trainer selects a problem for discussion, e.g., escape plan, and identifies one trainee to be the source of the problem.
(4) The role play is continued for about 20 minutes. During the role play, trainees who are role playing the staff try to resolve the problem. Trainees role playing the delinquents try to resist. Again, not all delinquents should be negative.
(5) After the role play is concluded, the trainer critiques it.

Module No. 13: Group interventions

Mode: Experiential

Goal: To teach trainees how to make interventions with an entire group and avoid making interventions with just a single person in the group

Comments: The importance of letting the group members work on each other should be emphasized. The trainer points out that delinquents will listen to each other before they will listen to an adult. Thus it is quite effective when the counselor directs the group to limit and lead.

Directions:

(1) The text in Chapter 2 pertaining to group interventions provides the basis of the training curriculum. This material is presented to the trainees.

(2) After presenting the training material, the trainer asks for four or five volunteers. Once again the trainer will role play the counselor and the volunteers will role play the group members. The trainer allows the trainees to role play a daily group session for 10 minutes. During this time, the trainer should try to use only the group interventions.

(3) The trainer stops the role playing after 10 minutes. The role play is discussed with the volunteers and other trainees. The trainer asks those involved in the role play to describe how they felt when the counselor made the interventions. The trainer points out that this type of intervention is subtle but strong.

(4) The trainer divides the trainees into small groups of no more than five persons. Each group should complete the worksheet in the Trainees' Workbook titled, *Making Interventions.* The trainer circulates among the groups to observe and make suggestions. The trainer redirects trainees to use the appropriate type of intervention.

(5) The small groups are disbanded and trainees reconvene into a large group. Trainees describe the exercise and receive feedback from the trainer.

Module No. 14: Resistance

Mode: Didactic

Goal: To teach trainees how to recognize the different ways that delinquents will resist treatment

Comments: Trainees must understand that delinquents are generally involuntary clients. That is, they do not seek out treatment on their own volition. Therefore, the successful group counselor must develop the ability to recognize the predictable ways in which delinquents will resist treatment.

Directions:

(1) The text in Chapter 2 pertaining to Resisting Change and Resisting Group Counselors is used as the basis of the training curriculum. The trainer lectures and provides examples based upon the text.

(2) When talking about *resisting change,* the trainer emphasizes the notion that a delinquent's loyalty to delinquent values is like some person's loyalty to country or religion.

(3) When talking about *resisting group counselors,* the trainer makes sure that trainees understand they will be the target of these resistance techniques. The trainer asks trainees how they might respond to various forms of resistance. The trainer evaluates the trainees' response in terms of the limit and lead

model. Other trainees also respond and evaluate responses based upon the limit and lead model.

Module No. 16: Limit and lead overview

Mode: Didactic

Goal: To help trainees begin to integrate the lectures and experiential training they have received

Comments: As trainees are ushered through the sequence of training exercises, they are exposed to a great deal of new information. It would not be unusual for a trainee to feel overwhelmed by the detail, complexity or amount of information presented during training. Therefore the trainer must provide an overview of the limit and lead group program. This overview should serve as a cognitive framework in which the trainees can assimilate the new information.

Directions:

(1) The trainer describes the limit and lead strategy in the context of the characteristics of delinquents.
(2) The trainer describes how Huddle-ups and Large Groups create a safe facility milieu. He/she underscores the notion that safety needs must be addressed prior to treatment needs.
(3) The trainer explains the function of Daily Groups as providing treatment. He or she emphasizes that Daily Groups meet different needs than do Called Groups.
(4) The trainer describes how the cognitive interventions can lead to lasting changes.
(5) The trainer answers questions and encourages trainees to state their overview of the group program, provides feedback, reinforces appropriate comments, and corrects erroneous views.

Module Nos. 17 and 18: Large Groups and Huddle-ups

Mode: Experiential

Goal: To allow trainees to practice the Large Group and Huddle-up techniques using all interventions presented during the training

Comments: Role play now focuses on integrating all previous training exercise.

Directions:

(1) The trainer divides the trainees into groups of five to six persons. He or she selects a topic likely to be raised by a delinquent youth. The trainer designates a counselor. Other trainees role play delinquent youth. The role play is allowed to last for 10 to 20 minutes. The trainer stops the role play after the allotted time and critiques it.

(2) The trainer assists role play as many times as possible in the time allowed. He or she ensures that all trainees have an opportunity to role play the counselor.

Module No. 19: Goals and philosophy of the program

Mode: Didactic

Goal: To conclude training on the limit and lead group program

Comments: This is the final training module. Like the conclusion in a Daily Group, it is an opportunity to highlight the most crucial issues and influence the trainees. It is important to keep it simple so that trainees can develop a common frame of reference for using the information. It must be recognized that, since this is the last module, it will be one of the more memorable modules.

Directions:

(1) Chapter 1 is used as the training curriculum. The trainer *must not* read the material to the trainees. He or she should be familiar enough with the material to be able to present it by using an outline.

(2) The trainer should refer to the Trainee Workbook for a summary of the goals and philosophy.

(3) The trainer discusses the goals and philosophy of the limit and lead group program. He/she indicates that the scientific literature supports this type of program. He or she cites the literature reviewed in Chapter 1.

(4) The trainer concludes by letting the trainees know that the goal of reduced recidivism is as attainable as it is important.

The preservice training exercises are designed to introduce the concepts of the limit and lead group programs and to allow trainees to practice the techniques that comprise the group program. The combination of teaching and role playing engages the trainees on cognitive and experiential levels. The optimal learning experience can be obtained by using this multimodal training approach. Trainees should be expected to begin conducting group sessions after completing the initial training. Naturally, trainees will need close supervision and the availability of ongoing in-service training. This is the topic of the next section.

ONGOING IN-SERVICE TRAINING

Those counselors undergoing this initial training should be able to recognize and use the fundamentals of the limit and lead group program. However, the experiences of the initial training will begin to fade over time. Trainees will forget some of the basics; therefore, follow-up training is necessary. Follow-up training can be provided by creating an ongoing in-service training program.

Before describing the in-service training program, a caution is in order. Training is *not* the answer to all problems that could occur in the group program. Sometimes a person is just not a good candidate to be a group counselor. If this is the case, training the person is a fruitless endeavor. Some people cannot be trained to be group counselors. If a person has received quality training and *still cannot* perform adequately, then a job reassignment may be in order. Another issue to be aware of is the competent counselor who does not hold group or who "does his own thing" in group. While individuality is fine, and the group training program allows for some flexibility, too much deviation from the program results in problems, and then this problem needs to be confronted. Training is not the intervention of choice in this situation. Rather, it is a management issue. The counselor's supervisor must hold the counselor accountable for executing his or her job duties. Failure to execute job duties when the counselor is competent and able should not lead to further training, it sould lead to personnel action.

As with the initial training, the structure of the in-service training is determined by learning objectives, training agendas, and training exercises. The experiential approach emphasized in the initial training is relied upon more heavily in the in-service training. The apprenticeship model of training is also retained as crucial. That is, an experienced counselor provides the training to less experienced counselors. The focuses of the training are the successes and failures that the trainee counselors experience as they conduct Called Groups and Daily Group.

The following are guidelines whereby an ongoing in-service training program can be implemented and maintained. Specific issues to be addressed in the training are not delineated. Rather, an attempt is made to describe a process that will generate training tailored to the specific needs of the trainees.

LEARNING OBJECTIVES

Learning objectives are easy to specify in the initial training. Trainees do not have an exposure to the limit and lead group program. Therefore, it is relatively easy to create learning objectives by simply requiring trainees to learn the concepts and the techniques of the program. Once a trainee has been through the initial training, the learning objectives should be based upon the trainee's specific needs. Specific training needs should be determined by observing the trainee and noting strengths and weaknesses. Training is devised that could reinforce strengths and remediate deficits. It's likely that there will be several group counselors at a facility. Training should be devised such that all counselors could receive In-Service Training as a group. To ensure that group training is relevant to all those involved in the training, two requirements should be met:

- A standard monitoring tool should be used when observing each counselor conduct group (see Appendix C).
- All counselors should be monitored at least once per month.

The importance of the use of a monitoring tool cannot be overestimated. First, the standard monitoring tool ensures fairness and equality when observing and evaluating counselors. The fairness of evaluations always emerges as an issue when two or more counselors are being evaluated. Second, the standard monitoring tool can identify common errors among counselors which can be meaningfully addressed in a group training session. The topics identified by the monitoring will be applicable to all those involved in the training. Consequently, motivation during the training is enhanced because trainees are working on common problems and issues.

Having an experienced counselor observe a trainee counselor once a month is a minimum requirement. More frequent observations are better. In fact, a monitoring schedule should be devised that allows for frequent observations of new counselors. Also, counselors experiencing problems in their group should be observed more often than once a month. An optimal approach is to create a quarterly monitoring schedule that dovetails with a quarterly in-service schedule.

TRAINING AGENDA

Issues to be addressed when preparing a training agenda include determining the training topic, the frequency of training, and the trainer. As stated previously, the training topic should be derived by monitoring all the counselors. Problems common to all counselors should be considered as training topics. It is important, however, to prioritize the potential training topics. Since it will be possible to address only one or two deficits in each session, those deficits representing the most serious threat to maintaining program integrity should be the focus of the training.

The frequency of in-service training needs to occur monthly after a program is established. New programs will need more frequent in-service training. It is recommended that counselors who recently completed the initial training receive weekly in-service training. These counselors can then be moved to a once-a-month training schedule as soon as they demonstrate an acceptable level of performance.

The trainer for the in-service program must always be an experienced group counselor. A staff development specialist without experience in the limit and lead group program or without experience in counseling delinquents would likely do more harm than good. The trainer must know how to answer the trainees' questions and respond to the many varied situations to arise in conducting group which could never be fully addressed in the initial training. The only way a person can ever attain the knowledge and credibility to conduct in-service training is to have prior experience as a group counselor. This is the apprenticeship model that was referenced earlier: Those with experience teach those who are new to the field.

TRAINING EXERCISES

An in-service training session should be 120 minutes in duration. The format of the training session should be similar to that of the training exercises presented in the initial training. The format is specified as follows:

(1) *Didactic.* The trainees are lectured on the issues and problems to be addressed during the session.
(2) *Model.* The trainer either role plays or shows a videotape that models the proper way to use the technique or intervention being taught.
(3) *Role Play.* The trainees are allowed to role play the technique and receive feedback.

Training in a group setting is very powerful. Trainees can learn by observation. They can also provide support and offer information about how they have successfully handled problems.

CHAPTER SUMMARY

A good training program relies upon a strong initial training that is supported by ongoing follow-up training. Counselors should not be left to struggle with a program that they perceive as foreign or complex. Training can offer the support needed for a successful group program. It is important, however, that training not be viewed as a panacea. Some issues are best addressed by training whereas others are best addressed by a personnel action. It does not usually require a great deal of acumen to determine which intervention is required. It may require a great deal of courage to act appropriately.

Problems may also arise in the course of training. When trouble-shooting problems, look to the trainer or the trainees to pinpoint the problem. Trainers may cause problems if they are unfamiliar with the material or the concepts. Problems may also occur if the trainer does not endorse the proposed model. Perhaps the most common source of trainer-related problems is using a trainer who is not a clinician. A professional trainer is no substitute for a person with good clinical experience. This is not to say that all clinicians make good trainers. That is simply not the case. Still, a good clinician who is a marginal trainer is going to be more effective than a professional trainer with no clinical experience.

The other source of problems that may arise during training are trainee-related. As in the case of trainer-related problems, there are countless possibilities for trainee-related problems. It is certainly beyond the scope of this book to delineate the problems and appropriate responses. It is, however, appropriate to offer a few guidelines. First trainers need to be aware that not all trainees are suited to be group counselors. Thus the trainer should be prepared to recognize and counsel with those trainees who do not appear appropriate for the training. Second, it is acceptable for a trainer to expel a trainee from a training session. This should occur in rare and extreme instances and should be followed up by counseling the trainee. Finally, the trainees may not endorse the group program. It may be something that is being forced upon them by their administration. In this situation, proceeding with the training would be ill advised. A group program cannot be better than those who use it. Training should only occur after there is clear administrative and front-line support for the program. Once again, training is crucial to the successful implementation and maintenance of the group program, but it can only be effective in the context of widespread support and acceptance.

Chapter 5

PREGROUP TRAINING FOR GROUP MEMBERS

The rationale for training youth to participate in the group program is quite simple: A youth trained to participate in therapy makes quicker progress and more progress than those youth who receive no training prior to treatment (Meichenbaum & Turk, 1987). It appears that the precounseling training impacts the youth in two ways: (a) based on the training, the youth develops realistic expectations and goals for treatment; and (b) the youth knows how to behave in counseling so as to maximize the effects of treatment. The underlying reasons for preparing a youth for treatment has to do with the skill level of the juvenile delinquent. As stated earlier, most delinquents have developed their street skills at the expense of their prosocial skills. Therefore, many delinquents will actually lack the specific skills necessary to benefit from treatment (Goldstein et al., 1986). Consequently, these youth must be trained so that they can acquire and use the appropriate group skills. This deficit in group-appropriate skills is perhaps the most important reason why these youth should receive pregroup training.

The method of pregroup training used in the limit and lead group program is the structured learning approach (Goldstein et al., 1980). Structured learning is an approach to skills training developed specifically for youth like juvenile delinquents who exhibit deficits in prosocial skills. The structured learning technique is based upon four steps:

Step 1: Modeling. An adult shows a videotape or engages in behavior that models the group counseling skill being taught to the youth.

Step 2: Role playing. At least two people engage in a role play designed to exhibit the group counseling skill.

Step 3: Performance feedback. After the role play is completed, all trainees discuss their impressions and observations.

Step 4: Transfer of training. Homework assignments are made so that the trainee must use the skills outside the training setting.

Using the structured learning approach, youth can begin to acquire the specific skills that would help them do well in group counseling. Most youth should be able to acquire the rudiments of the skill as a result of the structured learning instruction. It is expected that the youth will continue to refine these skills after being placed in the group program.

This chapter is organized as was the chapter on group counselor training. Learning objectives, the training agenda and training exercises are provided. Based upon this information, it should be possible to implement a pregroup training program for the youth who will participate in the limit and lead group counseling program.

LEARNING OBJECTIVES

The learning objectives are the specific goals to be obtained by the youth during the pregroup training. The goals of the pregroup training pertain to two specific areas: interpersonal skills necessary for interacting in group and knowledge necessary for the youth to follow the format for Called Groups and Daily Groups. The following are the learning objectives for the pregroup training.

INTERPERSONAL SKILLS

(1) To know the basics of group etiquette
(2) To know how to attend during group
(3) To know how to listen to what others say
(4) To know how to respond to feedback from others

GROUP KNOWLEDGE

(1) Called Groups
   • To know the format for Huddle-ups
   • To know the youth role during a Huddle-up
   • To know the format for a Large Group
   • To know the youth role during a Large Group
(2) Daily Groups
   • To know the format for the Daily Group

- To know how to do a self-report and assign the focus
- To know the problem-solving process
- To know about the offense cycle, victim empathy, and recidivism prevention

The learning objectives provide good criteria to evaluate the quality of a youth's learning experience. In fact, each youth should be tested on the basic how to's specified in the learning objectives.

TRAINING AGENDA

The training agenda is rather straightforward. There are 10 training exercises delineated in the next section. It is recommended that a youth be exposed to two training exercises per day, one in the morning and one in the afternoon. In this way, the pregroup training would be complete within five working days. Such a schedule could easily be accommodated into a one-week orientation program, which is quite common at many facilities.

TRAINING EXERCISES

The following training exercises are designed to prepare a youth to participate in the limit and lead group program. Specific group skills are taught, including interpersonal skills and group counseling skills. The training exercises are presented in outline form. The outlines conform to the structured learning model. Each outline can be conducted in a 40- to 60-minute session.

Topic: Group Etiquette

Goal: To train youth to recognize and use those behaviors that are acceptable in the group setting

Overview: Inform the youth that certain types of dress, language, and behavior are appropriate for group and some are not. Outline the appropriate behaviors.

(1) Proper dress
- The youth must wear shoes or slippers, pants, and shirt.
- No hats, tank tops, tube tops, or see-through clothing may be worn.
- The youth must be clean and groomed.

(2) Proper language
- Youth address the group counselor as Mr. or Ms.
- Youth address peers by their first name.
- No cursing.
- No addressing members or others as "dude," "homeboy," and so on.

(3) Sharing the floor
- Only one person talks at a time.
- If a youth wishes to say something, he or she raises his or her hand and waits to be called upon by the person who has the floor.

Model: It is recommended that a videotape be developed to show two types of groups: a group with etiquette and a group without etiquette.

Role Play: Four or five volunteers sit in a circle and demonstrate group etiquette. It is recommended that trainees *do not* role play a group without etiquette. Delinquents already know how to do this. Besides, once they start behaving this way it may be difficult for them to regain composure.

Feedback: Focus is on the benefits of an organized, well controlled group.

Homework: Trainer informs them that proper dress, language, and behavior will be required in all subsequent training sessions.

Topic: Attending

Goal: To teach youth behaviors that will result in the ability to pay attention

Overview: Attending is how a person pays attention. It is how a person knows what other people say or do. In a group session, it can show that the person is interested in what is being said and cares about the other person. The seated posture that shows that a person is attending in group is as follows.

(1) Youths maintain eye contact with the person speaking
(2) Youths sit with feet flat
(3) Youths sit with a forward lean
(4) Hands or forearms are on thighs
(5) Youths maintain an open posture—legs and arms are not crossed
(6) No distracting mannerism is allowed
(7) Youths remain relaxed

Model: The trainer puts two chairs in front of the group. A volunteer is seated in one while the counselor models how to attend. Then the volunteer is asked to model how to attend.

Role Play: The youth are paired-up. Each youth should attend to the other. Attending should occur for 30 to 60 seconds.

Feedback: The trainees are asked how much they could attend to. The trainer determines what they observed, being sensitive to issues about eye contact, e.g., staring each other down or challenge to fight by staring.

Homework: The youth are instructed to use attending skills throughout the day. At the next training session, they report on how well they attended. Discussion centers on the differences between the situations in which they attended and those in which they did not.

Topic: Listening

Goal: To increase the youth's ability to listen to what is being said and how it is being said.

Overview: Many people can listen without hearing a thing. A good listener can tell you what was said and how it was said. This is an important skill in group because group members must first be able to listen to another person before they can help. In order to be a good listener, group members need to pay attention to the following:

- *Content.* What is being said including the topic, reoccurring themes, and hidden agendas.
- *Style.* How the person talks including choice of words, volume, tone and rate of speech, and underlying feelings.

Model: One trainee is asked to come to the front of the class. The trainer engages the trainee in conversation. Afterward, the trainer reports back to the group what he/she heard when listening, using the following format:

(1) Content
- Topic
- Theme
- Agenda

(2) Style
  • Wording
  • Volume, tone and rate
  • Feelings

Role Play: The trainer asks for four volunteers. They are seated in a circle and told that they are going to engage in discussion of a topic. A topic relevant and pertinent to the youth (e.g., letters from home, release from the facility, and so on) is selected. They engage in a 5- to 10-minute discussion of this topic. Those trainees not involved in the role play should observe. After the role play, the previously presented format is used to critique the trainees' ability to listen. Input is elicited from all trainees.

Feedback: Feedback is not given on the role play but on the trainees' ability to listen. The youth who were good listeners are pointed out. If possible, the trainer tries to point out the strengths each youth may have. For example, some youth will be very good at picking out themes or hidden agenda. Other youth may be very good about responding to the style or manner in which a person speaks. To the extent possible, the trainer provides positive feedback.

Homework: The trainees are instructed to use their listening skills after the training session. At the beginning of the next training session, the trainer asks them to report on interaction during which they used the listening skills.

Topic: Responding

Goal: To teach youth how to react to a peer who is offering constructive criticism

Overview: Group counseling may occasionally entail discussing unpleasant topics. A natural reaction to discussing these topics may be a desire to run away or lash out against the person who is talking. Such a response will do little to help the person change. In fact, if a person uses the fight or flight response during group, it almost certainly means that constructive change is unlikely. Therefore, it is important for youth to learn how to respond to constructive criticism.

Model: The trainer tells the trainees that constructive criticism is a part of life. For example, employers evaluate employees and constructive criticism is a big part of it. A volunteer is requested. The trainer has the volunteer say one thing he likes and one thing he dislikes about the trainer. The trainer responds to the constructive criticism in an appropriate way.

Role Play: The trainer has the trainees pair up. If there is an odd number of trainees, the trainer can participate in the role play. The trainees are to engage in a structured discussion. First, each trainee states one thing that he or she likes and dislikes about him- or herself. Second, each trainee states one thing that he or she likes and dislikes about the other person. After the discussion is completed, each pair reports back to the group.

Feedback: As trainees are reporting the results of the discussion, the trainer asks: "How does it feel to compliment or criticize yourself? How does it feel when another person does it?"

After each trainee has had a chance to report, the reactions that they felt when criticized, i.e., fight or flight reactions, are discussed. Each trainee describes his or her strategy for not using the fight or flight response when receiving constructive criticism.

Homework: The trainees are instructed to use the responding skill outside of the session and to report back on the results of the use of the skill.

Topic: Delinquent Characteristics

Goal: To teach youth to recognize delinquent strengths and weaknesses

Overview: Even though many of the youth in pregroup training base their life upon the delinquent characteristics, they may not be able to recognize them. They may also not realize the harmful impact of these characteristics. Therefore the trainer has two crucial jobs. First, the trainer must didactically present each delinquent strength and weakness so that the youths can recognize them. Second, the trainer must underscore the irresponsible, exploitive impact of these characteristics. It is useful to contrast these characteristics with prosocial characteristics.

Model: First, the trainer presents an overview of the delinquent strengths and weaknesses. Then the trainer writes a few statements on the board and asks the trainees if they can recognize which delinquent characteristic it is based upon. After youths begin to be proficient at recognizing delinquent characteristics in the written form, the trainer presents them orally. That is, the trainer verbalizes some statements and the youth try to identify the underlying delinquent characteristic.

Role Play: The youth are divided into pairs. One youth attempts to verbalize delinquent characteristics while the other one listens and tries to identify them. After 5 minutes of role playing, the youth switch roles.

Feedback: After the role play, the trainer asks for feedback, reinforcing each youth's attempt to use his or her new knowledge.

Homework: The youth are instructed to observe others until the next session. At the next session, the youth give two examples of delinquent characteristics that they observed. One of the examples should pertain to their own behavior.

Topic: Huddle-ups

Goal: To teach youth how to use the Huddle-up Group to quickly solve problems

Overview: The purpose of the Huddle-up is to allow a peer to receive help and support from fellow peers. A Huddle-up is called by staff when a youth is having a problem that might become serious, e.g., a fight might occur. The staff calls for a Huddle-up to have the youth help their peer avoid this situation. The youth help by following the structure of the Huddle-up which is specified below:

(1) *Identifying the problem.* The problem is described by indicating who, what, when, and where.
(2) *Assign responsibility.* It is determined who must change so that the problem no longer continues.
(3) *Develop alternatives.* It is determined how the person must change in order to avoid the problem.
(4) *Conclusion.* It is indicated that a Huddle-up may be successful or unsuccessful. A successful Huddle-up is concluded when all present agree upon a specific course of action. Unsuccessful Huddle-ups conclude with no agreement. When this occurs, the issue is followed up in a Large Group or Daily Group.

Model: Videotape is an optimal way to model the Huddle-up Group. While it may be possible to model the Huddle-up using volunteers, it is likely that an appropriate model could not be produced. Therefore, it is highly recommended that a videotape be used during the modeling segment of training.

Role Play: Volunteers are requested. One youth is assigned to have a problem that would warrant a Huddle-up being called. The trainer role plays the staff person and the other youth role play positive, helpful peers. A description of the structure of the Huddle-up is on poster board or a blackboard. As the trainer moves the youth through the steps of the Huddle-up, reference is made to the description of the Huddle-up on the poster board. The role play should be repeated until all youth have had a chance to participate.

Feedback: After the role play, feedback is elicited from those involved in the role play by asking the following questions: (a) Was it difficult to follow the format? What was easiest? What was hardest?; and (b), did you feel helpful?

Those observing the role play could be asked to use their listening skills to describe what they observed.

Homework: Youth are expected to use the Huddle-up format and skills when called upon to do so.

Topic: Daily Group—Overview and Self-Report

Goal: To provide trainees with an overview of the Daily Group and to teach them how to make a self-report. Since the Daily Group is as important as it is complex, it will require three training sessions. In this first session, youth learn how to make a self-report.

Overview: The Daily Group is different from a Huddle-up. The Huddle-up is designated to eliminate problems. The Daily Group is designated to help youth understand a problem and change the things that are causing the problem. The Daily Group is structured in such a way that a youth can make lasting changes. The following is an outline of this structure.

(1) *Self-report.* Each group member gives a report on his or her behavior since the last meeting. The report focuses primarily on problems the youth has experienced. Positive experiences and contacts from family or friends are reported. The youth's peers listen to the report and fill in any missing information.

(2) *Assign the focus.* The group decides who most needs group on that day.

(3) *Problem solving.* The problem of a specific youth is addressed. The problem is described and an attempt is made to understand it. The problem is compared

to other problems in the youth's life to see if there are any common themes. An attempt is made to understand why the youth behaves as he or she does. Finally, alternatives are discussed and adopted as appropriate.

(4) *Conclusion.* Each group concludes with a summary of what was said and how it was said. Good conclusions require good listening skills.

Because the Daily Group format is so involved, it will be taught in several sessions. An overview has been provided. Attention will now be given to the self-report.

Model: Once again, the best model will be obtained by use of a videotape.

Role Play: Each youth is handed a pencil and writing pad. The trainer tells them to use these materials to make a few notes so that they can make a self-report. They are instructed to write their activities for the last 24 hours. The trainer has them divide their day into three segments: 12:00 a.m. to 12:00 p.m.; 12:00 p.m. to 6:00 p.m.; and 6:00 p.m. to 12:00 a.m. For each segment, a youth should specify:

• Problems with peers or staff
• Special accomplishments
• Contacts from family or friends

After the youths have completed their notes, they sit in a circle. Each youth gives a self-report using the notes that they wrote. Other youth listen and fill in any omissions.

Feedback: Feedback comes from two sources. Youth can describe how it feels to give a self-report or fill in omissions. The most important feedback will come from the trainer who reinforces good self-reports and offers constructive criticism on poor self-reports.

Homework: The youth are instructed to use the self-report when participating in a Daily Group.

Topic: Daily Group—Assigning Focus

Goal: To teach youth how to prioritize problems and determine who should be the focus of the group for that day

Overview: Based upon self-reports, the focus of the group sessions is decided. Since the purpose of the Daily Group is to get to the bottom of a problem and change it, it is rare when more than one problem can be addressed during a group. Therefore, the group members must carefully evaluate the need of each group member to have group that day. In evaluating the need of each group member, two questions should be asked: Who needs group the most? How long has it been since a person had group; has it been too long?

Since more than one person can appear to need group, problems are prioritized. The following is a priority listing of problems:

- Threat of harm or escape
- Offense cycle, victim empathy, or recidivism prevention worksheet
- Impending release or discharge

If two or more youth appear to need group, this priority list should be used to prioritize needs.

Model: The counselor uses a videotape of a Daily Group, which can accurately depict how to assign a focus.

Role Play: The counselor follows the instructions in the preceding lesson plan for self-reports. Each youth prepares a self-report. After the self-report is prepared, the youth sit in a circle and give the self-report. Then, going around the circle, each youth indicates whom they think most needs group. It may take several times around the circle before a focus can be determined. After the focus has been determined, the counselor moves to the feedback segment of the lesson but does not engage in problem solving. The youth are not prepared to do this. If a youth needs help with the problem identified during this lesson, he/she is referred to his/her counselor.

Feedback: Feedback elicited from the youth should focus on the effectiveness of the process. For example, the following questions could be asked:

(1) Did the right person get the focus of the group?
(2) Was the focus of the group tied to the self-report?
(3) Did the person who received group really need it? Was he or she ready to work on his or her problem?
(4) Were the priorities used?

Homework: Youth are instructed to use these skills when participating in Daily Group.

Topic: Daily Group—Problem Solving

Goal: To teach youths how to use the Daily Group problem-solving process

Overview: The person who becomes the focus of the group must try to understand and to resolve the identified problem. Although the problem-solving process may begin by focusing on a problem in daily living, the problem is related to other aspects of the youth's life. The purpose of this is to try to develop a rich understanding of the problem, which will lead to a long-term solution. The problem-solving process used in the Daily Group is outlined below. This outline should be presented didactically to the youths.

(1) *Identify the problem.* The problem that resulted in the person becoming the focus of the group is described in detail. To provide a detailed problem description, the who, what, when, where, and how of the problem is specified.

(2) *Acceptance of the problem.* The youth who is the focus of the group must accept the problem. He or she must own the problem and say that it is something he or she is willing to change or try to change.

(3) *Explain why the behavior is a problem.* Two problem areas of the behavior are identified.
   • Rules, regulations or norms that the behavior violates
   • The delinquent characteristics that act as the basis of the problem

(4) *Connect the problem to other problems.* An effort is made to determine if a pattern exists by seeing if the problem is similar to other problems that the youth has had. Any widespread occurrence of specific delinquent characteristics is identified.

(5) *Develop alternatives.* An alternative way of behaving is discussed. Emphasis is placed on developing new behaviors. An attempt is made simply to avoid telling a youth, "Do not do that." Any time a youth eliminates a behavior, he must develop a replacement behavior. This is the basis of the limit and lead model.

(6) *Follow-up.* A plan is developed to determine how well the youth is doing in the attempt to implement the alternative. The tone of the follow-up is crucial, i.e., be supportive. The youth is told not to expect to be perfect. The youth is told to expect some trouble implementing the behavior, and that follow-up is a way of providing support. Follow-up is not intended to blame or find fault.

Model: A videotape of an appropriate group problem-solving session is used.

Role Play: It would be too cumbersome to go through a self-report and assigning the focus. The youth are still in training, so it is important to keep things simple. Therefore, the role play should skip over the self-report and assigning the focus, and should begin with the problem-solving segment of group. The problem may be selected by asking for volunteers. If a youth volunteers with a serious and appropriate problem, then that problem may be used. If no one volunteers, then the trainer must make an assignment. As the trainees work on the problem, the trainer refers to the steps of the problem-solving process. It is best to have these steps outlined on a blackboard or poster board. As the group completes one step in the process the trainer allows them to move to the next. Youth are redirected when they use the problem-solving steps out of order. Working on the problem-solving process continues until each step has been completed.

Feedback: After the problem-solving session is completed, the outline of the problem-solving process is used to elicit feedback. Each step in the process is discussed. The trainees indicate how they think they did. This feedback session is used to teach and refine their skills. The trainer also helps them develop high expectations for their problem-solving abilities.

Homework: The youth are to begin using the problem-solving process in group and in individual counseling.

Topic: Group Therapy Worksheet

Goal: To teach youth how to complete a worksheet and then present it during a group session

Overview: As a supplement to the Daily Group, three written assignments will be completed by a youth. The assignments are intended to enhance the group experience. These three assignments are listed and defined below.

- *Offense cycle worksheet.* Description of how and why a youth engages in delinquent behavior
- *Victim empathy worksheet.* An exercise designed to increase a youth's awareness of the impact of a crime upon the victim(s)
- *Recidivism prevention worksheet.* A description of the ways a youth might plan to avoid recidivism.

Youth will have a chance to complete each of these worksheets during the course of treatment, so these worksheets will not be completed during pregroup training. In order to prepare a youth to use these worksheets, a

Personal History Worksheet will be completed during treatment. This will give the youth an opportunity to practice completing a worksheet.

Model: The trainer will complete several items on the Personal History Worksheet. After completing the first several items, the trainer will present this information to the group. As the trainer makes the presentation, an attempt is made to model how youth should present their personal histories in the group setting.

Role Play: The trainer gives each member of the group a Personal History Worksheet (Appendix D) and a pencil. The trainer instructs the trainees to complete the worksheet by providing a written answer to each item on the worksheet. The youth are allowed 10 to 15 minutes to work on the assignment. This is usually not enough time to complete the assignment, but it gives the youth enough to role play. As youth work on the assignment, the trainer should circulate among them. Many youth will need assistance in reading and writing.

After 10 to 15 minutes of working on the assignment, the trainer tells the trainees to stop and form a circle. The trainer begins going around the circle and each trainee presents one or two items on the worksheet. An effort is made to allow each youth an opportunity to make a presentation during the role play.

Feedback: After the role play, input is elicited by the following questions:

(1) Was it hard to respond to the questions?
(2) Were you cautious about revealing too much?
(3) Which questions were hard and which were easy?
(4) Was it helpful to have written material while making a presentation?

Homework: Youth are instructed to use this approach when completing other written group assignments. Youth are instructed to complete their Personal History Worksheet and be prepared to present it during a Daily Group session.

CHAPTER SUMMARY

The training curriculum for group members is both didactic and experiential. As such, it offers a powerful learning experience for a youth. It should be recognized, however, that most youth who participate in this program come from a background that almost guarantees they will not have the skills necessary to succeed in group counseling. Therefore it is unlikely that the 10 training modules will totally prepare a youth to participate in group counseling. It is advised that the training modules be considered necessary but not sufficient to ensure optimal performance. In addition to the training offered, new group members should receive feedback from their group counselor regarding the appropriateness of their behavior. The group counselor should help the new group members consistently use appropriate behaviors. One technique that has proven effective is to have posters made which outline the steps of the group process. These posters could be hung in the group room. It is also useful to make posters of the delinquent characteristics and display them in the group room. Such visual reminders are quite helpful and for some youths they are essential.

Chapter 6

DEVELOPING ADMINISTRATIVE SUPPORT

A group counseling program is just one of many programs and services that may be offered at a facility. A brief list of other rehabilitation services which could be offered at a facility include academic and vocational training; recreational, occupational and music therapy; drug and alcohol treatment; religious programs; and volunteer programs. This listing is certainly not exhaustive. It is quite possible for a facility to have many more services than those mentioned above. The point is that within a facility, many different programs often compete for personnel, physical space, and other resources.

One must also realize that the facility program occurs in the context of the facility's support services. Facility support services include food services, maintenance, personnel, and fiscal, to name but a few. The facility program must coordinate with the support services. For example, the fiscal department holds the purse strings that dictate whether or not the chairs, video equipment, handouts, and other supplies may be available for the group program. The food service department may have a set schedule for meals and snacks, which may impact the scheduling of group. The group program does not occur in isolation. It occurs in the context of the overall facility program and the facility's support services.

It is the task of a facility administrator to coordinate the varied programs and support services that may compete for the scarce resources of time, personnel, physical plant space, and money. It would be quite a relief for many facility administrators if there was a formula or set of instructions that could dictate just how to coordinate and administrate a facility program. Unfortunately, there are no such definitive instructions available. Instead, the facility administrator must be aware of and balance the demands of the program, the staff, the clients, and the resources available. Often, the administrator has little more to go on than a notion of the requirements for implementing and maintaining a rehabilitation service. Despite the administrator's best intentions, important aspects of a program may be compromised in an attempt to equitably distribute facility resources. When proper administrative support is not available, the quality of the facility's rehabilitation services is diminished. In fact, the unwitting or intentional lack of administrative support can undermine a facility program and negate the impact of qualified, dedicated, well trained staff.

Because proper administrative support is so crucial for implementing and maintaining a quality group program, guidelines for administrative support will be provided. These standards should be used by agency and facility administrators to ensure that the group program has proper administrative support. The standards that will be presented are based upon a number of principles and guidelines including: *Standards for Health Services in Juvenile Confinement Facilities* (NCCHC, 1984), *Standards for Health Services in Prisons* (NCCHC, 1987), *Standards for Juvenile Training Schools* (ACA, 1983), and *Standards for Psychology Services in Adult Prisons and Jails* (AACP, 1979).

AGENCY ADMINISTRATION

AGENCY TREATMENT AUTHORITY

The agency administrator should designate a single position as the Agency Treatment Authority. This position administrates the overall agency treatment program. The Agency Treatment Authority should have a Ph.D. in clinical psychology.

TREATMENT POLICY

The Agency Treatment Authority establishes policies pertaining to the agency treatment program. The policies outline the agency's treatment program including the treatment philosophy, treatment goals and objectives, and a mission statement.

MEETINGS AND REPORTS

The Agency Treatment Authority meets quarterly with Facility Treatment Authorities. Minutes of these meetings are maintained. The Agency Treatment Authority prepares quarterly statistical reports that summarize the types of treatment provided and their frequency for the entire agency. An annual report based upon quarterly statistical reports is provided. The annual report assesses whether or not the needs of the youth population are being met by existing services. Proposals are made to remediate deficits.

GOALS AND OBJECTIVES

A process of setting annual goals and objectives for treatment services is established by the Agency Treatment Authority. Goals and objectives are prepared by the Facility Treatment Authority and reviewed by the facility administrator and the Agency Treatment Authority. A semiannual update and annual review of goals and objectives are prepared by the Facility Treatment Authority and submitted to the facility administrator and Agency Treatment Authority.

BUDGET

The Agency Treatment Authority submits a budget for treatment services annually in accordance with agency guidelines. The reviewing agent accepts or denies budget requests and provides an explanation of any denials. Budget requests are relevant to facility treatment programs and are based upon the annual goals and objectives for the facility treatment services. The fiscal department should provide a cost-benefit report on each program operating in the agency. The data for this report should be gathered on an ongoing basis. The cost-benefit report should be prepared and distributed annually.

FACILITY ADMINISTRATION

FACILITY TREATMENT AUTHORITY

Each facility has designated a single Facility Treatment Authority with the responsibility for administrating the treatment program. The Facility Treatment Authority should be a Ph.D. clinical psychologist, a Master-level psychologist, or a social worker.

TREATMENT PROCEDURES

The Facility Treatment Authority is required to write or revise a manual of written policies and procedures pertaining to the treatment program. The manual should be used by new staff as an orientation device and by existing staff as a reference. The manual must be consistent with the agencywide policies written by the Agency Treatment Authority.

MEETINGS AND REPORTS

The Facility Treatment Authority meets with the facility administration at least monthly to discuss the treatment program. This meeting must be documented. At a minimum, the Facility Treatment Authority prepares a quarterly statistical report outlining the types of treatment provided and the frequency.

ORGANIZATIONAL STRUCTURE

A policy exists that delineates the facility's organizational structure. The organizational structure is such that the Facility Treatment Authority has direct supervision responsibility for all treatment staff.

TREATMENT SERVICES

INTAKE

Upon being committed to the agency, a youth shall receive a formal assessment that includes, but is not limited to, assessing psychological functioning, academic and vocational skills, health needs, and family and social histories. A written plan must exist that specifies how assessment data can be used for treatment planning and long-term case management.

TREATMENT APPRAISAL

Upon admission to a facility, the youth is interviewed by the treatment staff. The intake data is reviewed. An initial treatment plan and initial program assignment is made at this time. A written plan must exist showing how appraisal information leads to treatment planning.

MENTAL HEALTH TREATMENT

This type of treatment entails services for youth with a psychiatric crisis or a psychiatric diagnosis. A written policy exists that requires staff to inform youth about how to access mental health services providers. The policy indicates the manner in which youth will request and gain access to these services.

SPECIAL SERVICES

PROGRAM DEVELOPMENT

A written policy exists, which guides the development of special counseling services. The Agency Treatment Authority and the facility administrator share the responsibility of reviewing and approving proposals for special counseling services.

CRISIS INTERVENTION

A written policy is developed by the Agency Treatment Authority, which delineates the assessment and disposition of youth in crisis. As warranted, criteria and guidelines should be developed that indicate when and how to transfer youth in crisis to a mental health facility. A log is maintained to document all crisis intervention activity. Crisis intervention activity is communicated to the administration, other departments, and across shifts.

BEHAVIOR MANAGEMENT

Specific procedures are established for managing predatory, suicidal, and self-mutilative youth. The procedures are not punitive and are designed to remediate the problem behavior. The procedure limits the use of physical force and physical or chemical restraint.

CONSULTATION

The Facility Treatment Authority consults with the facility administrator about disciplinary actions, transfers, program assignments, and housing assignments for youth with psychological disorders.

PROGRAM INTEGRATION

CONTINUITY OF CARE

A written policy exists, which delineates the way intake data is used in treatment planning and long-term case management. Each youth has a treatment plan, which documents the services rendered and the rationale for selecting each service.

PROGRAM DESCRIPTION

There is a comprehensive description of each facility's treatment program. The description includes, but is not limited to, the following program components: Called Groups, Daily Groups, Special Groups, behavior management programs, and crisis intervention programs.

SCHEDULING

A comprehensive program schedule is developed such that program activities do not compete for time or space. Daily Groups are scheduled for 60 to 75 minutes, five days a week.

STAFFING

Program staff review each youth's performance in the program at least every 90 days. The group counselor chairs the staffing committee. Direct-care staff and the youth participate in the staffing. The staffing is documented in the youth's file. The Facility Treatment Authority audits 10% of all staffings quarterly.

DISCHARGE PLANNING

A plan is developed for each youth, which helps the youth maintain changes made during counseling.

QUALITY ASSURANCE

INTERNAL QUALITY ASSURANCE

A written policy exists delineating how treatment services will be monitored and who will conduct the monitoring. Each group counselor should be observed conducting group at least once per month.

STANDARD MONITORING DEVICE

When observing group counselors, objective criteria should be incorporated into a standard monitoring device used when observing all counselors.

REMEDIAL PROGRAMS

Using the information generated by the quality assurance activities, remedial programs for staff should be instituted. Remedial programs include scheduled training activities and individual training activities for counselors with specific problems.

PERSONNEL

LICENSURE

Facility treatment providers must possess the same licensure, certification or registration requirements that providers in the community must possess to provide the same services. The facility administration must verify the licensure of each service provider working at the facility.

JOB DESCRIPTIONS

A written job description must exist for all those providing treatment. The job descriptions must be approved by the Agency Treatment Authority. Group counselors should not be assigned tasks that interfere with counseling duties.

CAREER LADDER

A career ladder for counselors must be created. The career ladder must be comprised of at least three steps. Each step must allow for increasing salary. The career ladder for counselors must be commensurate with the career ladder for administrators.

ALLOCATION OF POSITIONS

A sufficient number of group counselor positions should be made at each facility. The ratio of group counselors to youth should not exceed 1:16. There should be one trained group counselor substitute for every two group counselors.

SUPERVISION

Staff required to supervise group counselors must be qualified professionals with experience in conducting group counseling.

EVALUATION

An annual evaluation of the group counselor's performance is conducted. The evaluation is based partially upon group monitoring conducted by the Facility Treatment Authority. Merit raises, promotions, and disciplinary action must be largely determined by the person's performance as a group counselor.

TRAINING

INITIAL TRAINING

A written training curriculum exists, which can be used to train new group counselors. The Agency Treatment Authority must approve the curriculum and update it annually. The training curriculum must offer at least 24 hours of initial training specifically about group counseling. Group counselors must complete the initial training prior to being allowed to conduct group counseling.

IN-SERVICE TRAINING

In-service training for group counselors is conducted at least monthly. The in-service training is conducted by The Facility Treatment Authority. In-service training topics should be selected based upon the needs of the group counselors. In-service training sessions should be one to two hours in duration. For new group counselors, in-service must occur on a weekly basis. Experienced group counselors receive in-service training at least monthly.

SUPERVISORY TRAINING

The Facility Treatment Authority must receive at least 16 hours of continuing education annually. Valid training topics must pertain to clinical supervision or counseling techniques and issues.

FACILITY ORIENTATION

All staff other than group counselors must receive an orientation regarding the philosophy, goals, and mission of the group program. These staff members include direct child-care workers and support staff. These staff members must also receive information about changes made in the group program.

LIBRARY

Each facility should have a library of counseling books, journals, and videos. The Facility Treatment Authority is responsible for acquiring and supervising the distribution of materials.

RESOURCE MANAGEMENT

ANNUAL ASSESSMENT

The Facility Treatment Authority conducts an annual assessment of the resources allocated to the treatment program. Recommendations are made for modification of existing resources.

CLINICAL SPACE

Sufficient space is allocated for the maintenance of the group counseling program. Equipment requirements should also be considered as important, e.g., tests, chairs, video equipment, and other necessary supplies.

CHAPTER SUMMARY

The guidelines presented in this chapter are broad. As such, they may encompass a variety of different programs, not just the limit and lead group program. In this sense, the guidelines are generic. An agency or facility administrator could use these guidelines as audit criteria to evaluate an existing group program. The results of the audit could evince the strengths and the weaknesses of an existing program. Upon discovery of weaknesses, plans for remediating the group program could be developed and implemented. The results would be an overall improvement in the quality of services offered to the youth in the program. This is, after all, the primary purpose of this book: to promulgate a method for conducting group counseling, which creates a powerful therapeutic experience that has a long-term impact on the behavior of the youth.

Appendixes

Appendix A

LIMIT AND LEAD GROUP COUNSELING
Trainee Workbook

INTRODUCTION

The Trainee Workbook is a supplement to the book, *Group Counseling with Juvenile Delinquents*. The workbook contains material that mirrors the material found in the book. There are two basic types of material in the Trainee Workbook. First, there is material that summarizes the important points covered in the training. This material serves as a learning aid to trainees. Second, the Trainee Workbook contains questions and discussion material that allows the trainees to use the information being presented. The underlying purpose is to facilitate learning. It is assumed that if the trainees have to use the information, they will learn it better.

PERSONAL REPORT

NAME: _____   TITLE: _____

FACILITY: _____

YEARS AT FACILITY: _____ PREVIOUS POSITIONS: _____

_____

_____

PREVIOUS CHILD CARE JOBS: _____

_____

_____

_____

MARITAL STATUS: _____   NUMBER OF CHILDREN: ___

EDUCATION: _____

_____

_____

PREVIOUS GROUP LEADER TRAINING: _____

_____

_____

_____

LIFE EXPERIENCES WHICH PREPARE YOU TO WORK WITH

DELINQUENTS: _____

_____

_____

_____

REASON WHY YOU CURRENTLY WORK WITH DELINQUENTS: _____

_____

_____

APPENDIX A: TRAINEE WORKBOOK

WHAT DO YOU THINK DELINQUENTS NEED TO DO OR EXPERIENCE IN

ORDER TO LEAD A PRODUCTIVE LIFE? _____

_____

_____

_____

WHAT DO YOU HOPE TO GAIN FROM THIS TRAINING? _____

_____

_____

_____

CHARACTERISTICS OF DELINQUENT YOUTH

Delinquency is a life-style. The more delinquent characteristics possessed by a youth, the more severe the delinquency. Youth with many delinquent characteristics have a life-style of exploiting and harming others.

DELINQUENT STRENGTHS

These characteristics enable the youth to take advantage of others:

- *Power play.* Manipulation and domination
- *Fronting.* Secrets and lies
- *Energy.* Mental and physical activity
- *False pride.* Entitlement and ownership
- *Corrosion.* Cannot keep commitments

DELINQUENT WEAKNESSES

These are the positive skills that the delinquent has not developed because the delinquent strengths work too well.

- *Responsibility.* Self-starter who does what is "right"
- *Empathy.* Knows how others feel and considers it before acting
- *Thinking.* Poor learning and memory
- *Counterdependence.* Not independent but not dependent
- *Internal Control.* Cannot tolerate tension

STRENGTH OF ADOLESCENCE

Adolescents possess strengths that enable them to change more readily than adults.

- *Adaptability.* Personality is not fixed
- *Imitation.* Learns by imitating
- *Values.* A time for developing morals
- *Intimacy.* A willingness to experiment with closeness

DISTINGUISHING DIFFERENT TYPES OF CHARACTERISTICS

(1)   The following are statements made by delinquents. Determine which delinquent characteristic is being exhibited.

DELINQUENT CHARACTERISTIC

- "I know that I will not get caught. I am too clever. Everyone else is stupid compared to me."   _____

- "Nobody tells me what to do. I am in charge of myself, I do not need anybody."   _____

- "I like thinking about doing crimes. It is exciting."   _____

- "Most people do not care if I rip them off. Everyone gets ripped off once in a while."   _____

- "I will get revenge because you should not have done that to me."   _____

(2)   Give examples of the following types of characteristics.

- Corrosion: _____

     _____

- Fronting: _____

     _____

- Internal control: _____

     _____

- Thinking problems: _____

     _____

(3)   The strengths of adolescents include adaptability, imitation, value development, and intimacy. Which one of these do you think is the most potent strength? Explain.

     _____

     _____

LIMIT AND LEAD STRATEGY

The following are samples of different behaviors that frequently occur when conducting group counseling with juvenile delinquents. Using the limit and lead strategy, indicate how you would respond to each behavior. Remember, limit responses are designed to stop negative behavior. Lead responses are designed to teach or reinforce positive behavior. Indicate which response is appropriate for each of the items listed below.

(1)   One group member comes in late to group. A few group members are dressed inappropriately. Most members seem distracted and inattentive.

(2)   A youth begins to cry as he talks about missing home.

(3)   Two group members begin telling stories about how much fun they had using drugs.

(4)   A group member gets angry at another group member for not paying attention.

(5)   A group member stands up to leave because he is feeling anxious.

(6)   A group member is using hand signals to control who talks and for how long.

(7)   A group member is trying to describe his feelings. He is having a difficult time. Other group members try to help him put his feelings into words.

(8)   A group member curses a peer. He challenges the group counselor to do something about it.

(9)   A group member begins destroying furniture in the group room.

(10)   A group member states that the entire group should have a vacation from group since they are doing so well.

The basic strategy for treatment with delinquents is limit and lead. Limits are put on the youth's negative behaviors, i.e., delinquent strengths. The counselor leads the youth toward more appropriate behavior, e.g., helps the youth remedy delinquent weaknesses.

Good limit setting requires that the limits be specific, clearly stated, consistently enforced and fair.

Good leading behavior entails the use of positive reinforcement for steps taken toward appropriate behavior.

GUIDELINES FOR DAILY GROUPS

SELF-REPORT

Each youth takes a turn and reports on problem behaviors since the last session. No excuses or explanation are offered. Group members listen to the report and correct the youth for distortions or deletions. The group counselor checks the log and speaks with other staff prior to the session so that he/she can ensure the youth gives a full report.

The group counselor can give the report using school reports or daily logs. This is not the ideal and should only happen if the group is new or negative.

ASSIGNING THE FOCUS

Based upon the self-report, a focus is assigned to the session. Because the problem-solving process is very involved, it is best not to deal with more than two problems in a session. The focus is assigned based on who most needs the session and who can most benefit from it.

Youths assign the focus by voting on who should be the focus. The group counselor can break deadlocks.

PROBLEM SOLVING

This is the most important part of the session. This is the time when a youth begins to understand and change delinquent behavior. There are six steps in the problem-solving process.

(1) *Identify the problem.* Describe the who, what, when, where and how.

(2) *Acceptance of the problem.* The youth accepts responsibility for the problem.

(3) *Explain why the behavior is a problem.* The youth states why the behavior is negative and identifies underlying delinquent characteristics.

(4) *Connect the problem to similar problems.* The youth looks at his past and present life to determine if a pattern of problems exists.

(5) *Develop alternatives.* The youth develops and enacts a plan whereby the negative behavior can be replaced by positive behavior.

(6) *Follow-up.* A method for evaluating the plan's effectiveness is developed.

CONCLUSION

A youth may summarize the group. The counselor concludes by teaching, labeling, and reinforcing. The fours steps of teaching are: (a) confront negative delinquent behavior in an open and honest way; (b) interpret underlying goals and motives of youths; (c) identify patterns of negative behavior and connect it with delinquent characteristics; and (d) predict how the future will look if the youth does not change.

DAILY GROUPS WORKSHEET

SELF-REPORT

(1)   What information must be gathered by the counselor prior to the session?

_____

(2)   Identify a common problem of the self-report and describe how you would handle it.

_____

_____

ASSIGNING THE FOCUS

(1)   Rank order the following problems to determine which one you would address first, second, third, and forth.

_____   Jerry had a fight in the cafeteria this morning.

_____   Steffany and Beth are planning to escape in two days.

_____   John is ready to present his Recidivism Worksheet.

_____   The entire cottage has been horseplaying all day.

PROBLEM SOLVING

Think about a problem that you recently encountered in your personal life. It does not have to be a big problem, it just has to be personal. Using the problem-solving format, try to solve your problem.

- Identify the problem. _____

_____

- Accept problem. _____

_____

- Explain why it is a problem. _____

_____

- Connect to other problems. _____

_____

- Develop alternative. _____

_____

- Follow-up. _____

_____

(1)   Is this process useful? _____

(2)   What is the most difficult part of this process? _____

_____

(3)   What is the most useful part of the process? _____

_____

OFFENSE CYCLE WORKSHEET

1. Recall an offense you committed. Describe it. _____

   _____

   _____

2. *Negative event.* What negative event occurred prior to this offense? _____

   _____

   _____

3. *Negative thinking.* What negative thoughts did you have about the event? _____

   _____

   _____

4. *Negative feeling.* Describe how the negative event made you feel

   _____

   _____

5. *Urge to offend.* What fantasies did you have about offending? _____

   How did the fantasies make you feel? _____

   _____

   _____

6. What planning did you do before the offense? _____

   _____

   _____

7. How did you feel during and immediately after the offense? _____

   _____

   _____

8. Describe any negative feelings you have after the offense. _____

   _____

   _____

9. What, if any, promises did you made to reform? _____

   _____

_____

10. What needs are you really meeting when you commit your offense? _____

_____

_____

11. List other ways you can meet these same needs. _____

_____

_____

OFFENSE CYCLE SUMMARY WORKSHEET

As you look over your offense history, you should be able to determine if a pattern exists. The easiest way to see the pattern is to identify the events, feelings, or thoughts occurring most frequently in your offense cycle. In the space below, list the top three items in each of the categories. The top items are determined by simply recalling and listing the parts of your offense cycle for three separate offenses.

NEGATIVE EVENT

(1) _____

(2) _____

(3) _____

NEGATIVE FEELING

(1) _____

(2) _____

(3) _____

NEGATIVE THINKING

(1) _____

(2) _____

(3) _____

ACTS

(1) _____

(2) _____

(3) _____

THOUGHTS AND FEELINGS AFTER THE OFFENSE

(1) _____

(2) _____

(3) _____

GUIDELINES FOR HUDDLE-UPS

NEED FOR A HUDDLE-UP

- Overt aggression or threat of overt aggression
- Flagrant violations of the rights of others and failing to respond to staff confrontation
- Serious challenges to staff authority which may lead to a physical confrontation
- Escape or attempted escape

INITIATING A HUDDLE-UP

- Only staff may initiate a Huddle-up. Any youth may *request* a Huddle-up, but staff must initiate it. Staff must know members before initiating. Members of the group must be positive and willing to confront if the Huddle-up is to be effective.

IDENTIFY THE PROBLEM

- Identify the problem, i.e., who, what, when, where, and how.
- Label the behavior as problematic, i.e., why the behavior is inappropriate for the situation.

ASSIGN RESPONSIBILITIES

The troubled youth accepts responsibility for the behavior.

DEVELOP ALTERNATIVES

- The troubled youth agrees not to continue with the behavior.
- The individual is required to set a specific goal.
- The troubled youth develops an alternate behavioral plan.
- The youth commits to the alternative behavior.

CONCLUSION

- The group is formally concluded and the youth is given consequences if the group has solved the problem.
- Concluding the group is delayed if the problem is unsolved or the group has behaved inappropriately.
- To conclude the group, the events are summarized.

(1) The problem behavior is restated along with the reason why it was a problem and what the troubled youth will do as an alternative.

(2) Positive behaviors exhibited by individuals or the group are reinforced.

HUDDLE-UPS

(1) Give examples of the various situations which necessitate a Huddle-up.

- Overt aggression or threat of same

_____

_____

- Flagrant violation of rights

_____

_____

- Serious challenges to staff

_____

_____

(2) Give examples of situations that do not require a vigorous intervention such as a Huddle-up.

- Possible aggression

_____

_____

- Violating rights

_____

_____

- Defiance

_____

_____

(3) Ed and John begin verbally challenging each other during math class. It has become obvious that neither youth will back down. An aggressive outburst seems obvious. You initiate a Huddle-up. Respond to the following.

- Identify the problem(s).

_____

_____

- Describe your goal for this group.

_____

_____

- What is your conclusion criteria?

_____

_____

(4) Alana has been horseplaying despite staff instructions to the contrary. Alana seems to be escalating. She has destroyed personal property of others. It appears that serious physical harm to others is inevitable. You initiate a Huddle-up.

- Identify the problem(s).

_____

_____

- Describe your goal for this group.

_____

_____

- What is your conclusion criteria?

_____

_____

CHARACTERISTICS OF EFFECTIVE GROUP COUNSELORS

COMMITMENT

The counselor must have a personal desire to work with youth in general and juvenile delinquents in particular. The commitment must be strong as it is the basis of the motivation to work with delinquents.

RESPONSIBILITY

The counselor must meet all professional and personal obligations. The responsible counselor is a role model and often a sharp contrast to other adults in the delinquent's life.

INTENSITY

The counselor must be able to gain and hold the delinquent's attention. This is done by exhibiting tenacity and persistence in the counseling relationship.

SKEPTICAL

Given the delinquent's tendency to front and pretend, the counselor must believe nothing and doubt everything. All judgment is suspended. The counselor must remain curious. The counselor never falls into the trap of leaving well enough alone.

LEADERSHIP

The counselor must be a leader. To a large extent, this entails confronting negative acts and reinforcing prosocial behavior. The counselor must be confrontive and advocate prosocial values. A nondirective counselor may actually promote delinquent behavior.

COUNSELOR CHARACTERISTICS WORKSHEET

The counselor characteristics as presented in the training may seem abstract. It is important that the counselor be able to translate these abstractions into concrete behaviors. In the space below list some behaviors that could represent each of the counselors characteristics. List behaviors as they might be exhibited in a formal counseling session or during informal contact.

Commitment.

_____

_____

_____

_____

Responsibility.

_____

_____

_____

_____

Intensity.

_____

_____

_____

_____

Skeptical.

_____

_____

_____

_____

Leadership.

_____

_____

_____

_____

USING INTERVENTION

(1) A youth has a history of sadness and being withdrawn. He rarely speaks in group. Today in group he is bragging about his committing an offense. What do you say to the youth?

_____

_____

_____

(2) You have identified a youth as a negative leader. He is sitting in group giving hand signals to peers indicating who can talk and when. What do you do?

_____

_____

_____

(3) The group tries to confront a peer but the peer's defenses are too strong. The peer is able to project the blame from his problems. It appears that he is going to avoid dealing with the problem. What do you say?

_____

_____

_____

(4) Identify the following types of interventions.

    (a) Let us not be concerned with that right now. Let us return
        to Johnny's anger issue.   _____

    (b) Why do you suppose people steal?   _____

    (c) I agree with what you say.   _____

    (d) The reason you hit Tony is that you were confronted earlier
        by staff.   _____

    (e) Do you realize you look at Johnny every time before
        answering?   _____

    (f) That type of thinking is "delinquent thinking."   _____

    (g) I would suggest that horseplaying is a way for you to
        intimidate others.   _____

    (h) How many times have you done that?   _____

    (i) Have you tried counting to 10 before responding?   _____

    (j) Do you realize that when Tony tries to talk, you always
        interrupt?   _____

TWELVE INTERVENTIONS

Specific interventions have specific effects on the youths. Some interventions limit and some lead. Counselor interventions that lead the youth include approval, delay, closed questions, reflection, clarification, and open-ended questions. Counselor interventions that limit the youth include developing alternatives, redirection, labeling, confrontation, interpretation, and expulsion.

	When to use	*Counselor's Goal*
Minimal Lead Approve Delay Closed question	These interventions are used when the group is caring, supportive, and working well.	The group is allowed to work. Members are allowed to become more cohesive.
Moderate Lead Reflection Clarification Open question	These interventions are used to force a group to go into more depth, and to make the discussion refocused and positive.	The group is taught to be more effective. "Hot" issues are not allowed to be avoided.
Moderate Limit Develop alternative Redirection Labeling	These interventions are used when the group is willing to work but has not yet developed positive values.	Tthe group is taught the difference between right and wrong. They are taught to behave accordingly.
Large Limit Confrontation Interpretation Expulsion	The group is out of control. Strong counselor action is required.	Limits are set and it is demonstrated that only positive behavior is acceptable.

REMEMBER

- The counselor who can use all the interventions is the most sophisticated.
- The counselor who develops a sense of timing with these interventions is the most skillful.
- The same intervention has a different effect on different youth.

VICTIM EMPATHY WORKSHEET

Recall a crime that you committed. With this crime in mind, answer the following questions. The purpose of this exercise is to consider how your behavior affected the life of the person whom you offended.

(1) Describe the crime you committed. _____

_____

_____

_____

(2) Who was your victim? _____

_____

_____

_____

(3) What did your crime cost the victim?

Financially _____

_____

Emotionally _____

_____

(4) How did your crime affect the victim's family and friends? _____

_____

_____

_____

(5) How has the crime affected the rest of the victim's life? _____

_____

_____

_____

(6) How would you feel if the crime had been committed against you? _____

_____

_____

_____

(7) What do you think should happen to persons who commit this type of crime? _____

_____

_____

_____

(8) Are you paying too much or too little for this crime? _____

_____

_____

RECIDIVISM PREVENTION WORKSHEET

It is very difficult to successfully complete a therapy program. If you do success-fully complete the program, there are no guarantees that the changes you make in treatment will be lasting changes unless you actively prepare to face the situations and events that can cause you to slide back into the old ways of thinking, feeling, and behaving. This backsliding is known as a recidivism. Recidivism is a process that unfolds over a period of time. A generic recidivism process looks like Figure AP.2.

Negative event → Dangerous decisions → High-risk situations → Lapse (urge or gantasy) → Low self-esteem → Recidivism

In the space below, personalize the recidivism process by describing how you might enact each step in the recidivism process. Think about your past offenses and how each step in the offense might actually have looked in the context of the recidivism process.

- Negative event (triggers)_____

  _____

  _____

- Dangerous decisions _____

  _____

  _____

- High-risk situations _____

  _____

  _____

- Lapse (urge or fantasy) _____

  _____

  _____

- Low self-esteem _____

  _____

  _____

RECIDIVISM PREVENTION SUMMARY WORKSHEET

This worksheet builds upon the initial Recidivism Prevention Worksheet. Take the information on that worksheet and place it in the middle column. Then fill in the information for each step in the relapse process for the different time frames. This exercise is designed to emphasize the fact that recidivism is a process that unfolds over time—sometimes a period of months.

	Initial	*Middle*	*End*
Negative events			
Dangerous decisions			
High-risk situations			
Lapses			
Low self-esteem			

GUIDELINES FOR LARGE GROUPS

Large groups are problem-solving groups that involve all youth in a living environment. Large Groups are called in response to dangerous situations that threaten the welfare of all those in the living environment. Large Groups are used to prevent harm and ensure safety.

NEED FOR A LARGE GROUP

- A weapon is known or suspected to be in the facility.
- A tool used for escape is suspected or discovered.
- An escape or assault plan has partially surfaced.
- An increase in physical or sexual assault.
- Contraband is discovered.

CONDUCTING A LARGE GROUP

- Preplan the entire process. Assign roles to staff. Anticipate obstacles.
- Assemble all staff and youth.
- Introduce the issue to be solved. Begin using the problem-solving format.
- Keep the members focused.
- Take breaks every 90 minutes. Use the break time constructively.

MAKING INTERVENTIONS WITH THE GROUP

(1) You are conducting a group and the following situations arise that require redirection. How would you respond?

   • The group wants to talk about the camping trip they will go on this weekend.

   Redirection: _____

   _____

   • The group awards the focus to a scapegoat. You know there are important issues to be addressed.

   Redirection: _____

   _____

   • A member is talking about being physically abused by a parent. Members begin to become anxious. Some try to bring up other topics.

   Redirection: _____

   _____

(2) Process comments reach beneath the surface and address the reason youth behave the way they do. How could you make process comments in the following situations?

   • The group refuses to allow a member to talk about being physically abused by a parent.

   Process comment: _____

   _____

   • Group members seem distracted and nonsupportive. There is little participation.

   Process comment: _____

   _____

   • A member dominates the session by bringing out his problems but refuses to accept the help of others.

   Process comment: _____

   _____

(3) You need to be able to side-step challenges to your authority. How would you counterattack these statements group members make to you or about you?

   • You never let us have any fun. Why can we not talk about neat stuff in group?

   Counter: _____

   _____

   • Why do you not tell us what you would do if a cop hit you? I will bet you were no angel when you were growing up. Come on, tell us one bad thing that you did.

   Counter: _____

   _____

   • Why do I have to go to bed before the Level IVs? I am a Level III. Can I stay up late?

   Counter: _____

   _____

DELINQUENT DEFENSES

The delinquent tries to resist changing. When resisting change is not totally effective, the delinquent may resist the group counselor directly. The delinquent's defenses for resisting change and group counselors are listed below.

RESISTING CHANGE

Silence. Does not respond or does not speak for fear of being held accountable.

Agreement. May fake agreement or being positive even though that is not how he/she really feels.

Rejection. Peers who begin to change and adopt prosocial values are rejected.

Avoidance. Prosocial adults and peers are viewed as dangerous and, consequently, are avoided.

Victim stance. Blaming others for one's problem or viewing oneself as a victim when this is not true is victim stance.

RESISTING GROUP COUNSELORS

Emotional sabotage. This is trying to get the group counselor emotionally aroused so as to obstruct progress.

Counterattack. This is when a youth points out the faults of others when his/her own faults are pointed out.

Double jeopardy. This is refusing to answer for the same issue twice.

Demands. Unrealistic demands are made that cannot or should not be met.

GOALS AND PHILOSOPHY OF THE GROUP PROGRAM

There are two distinct goals of the group program:

- *Goal for the individual.* Help the individual eliminate harmful, exploitive behavior and replace it with positive, appropriate behavior.
- *Goal for the group.* Create a safe, secure living environment characterized by people who care about each other.

Based on these two goals, a philosophy for the group program emerges. Simply stated, the philosophy of the group program is that youths can be positive members of society when they are taught positive skills and they see adults modeling positive skills. It is recognized that youths will need to be confronted and limits will need to be set and enforced on behavior that is harmful. Further, it is recognized that all youths in the living environment must take responsibility for maintaining a safe and secure environment. Still, the overriding concern is for the individual. The individual must be helped to set goals and develop a vision about the future. All work that occurs in the group program should be designed to help the youth attain these goals.

Appendix B

GROUP LEADER TRAINING POSTTEST

GROUP LEADER TRAINING POST TEST

Name: _____   Date: _____

Facility: _____   Title: _____

GOALS AND PHILOSOPHY

- The goal for individual youths in the group program is _____

  _____

- The goal of the group for the living environment is _____

  _____

- The philosophy of the group program is _____

  _____

CONCEPTUAL FOUNDATION

T   F
☐   ☐   1. Anyone under 18 years of age who breaks the law is a juvenile delinquent.

☐   ☐   2. We can accurately categorize different types of delinquents.

☐   ☐   3. A *power play* is characterized by the delinquent's willingness to dominate others.

☐   ☐   4. *Fronting* means that the delinquent is not open and honest.

☐   ☐   5. Energy allows the delinquent to be positive.

☐   ☐   6. Most delinquents do not have unrealistic pride.

☐   ☐   7. *Corrosion* means that the delinquent does not stick to commitments.

☐   ☐   8. Most delinquents are sympathetic and sensitive to others.

☐   ☐   9. Most delinquents have trouble learning by observing others.

☐   ☐   10. *Counterdependence* means the delinquent is neither independent nor dependent.

☐   ☐   11. Delinquents reject those who are responsible.

☐   ☐   12. Delinquents will distract the counselor by trying to arouse intense emotions.

☐   ☐   13. "If he did not want the car stolen, he should not have left the keys in it." This is an example of victim's stance.

☐   ☐   14. Most adolescents are adaptive and can change easily.

☐   ☐   15. Most adolescents can learn by imitating.

☐   ☐   16. Two characteristics of effective group counselors are harshness and firmness.

☐   ☐   17. *Skepticism means doing the right thing.*

T   F

☐ ☐ 18. A common group counselor mistake is trying to be friends, or "one of the boys," with the delinquents.

☐ ☐ 19. Ultimately, the group counselor wants the youths to run the group.

☐ ☐ 20. A single intervention has a different effect on different youths.

Answer the following questions by giving brief responses.

(1) Describe the limit and lead strategy. _____

_____

(2) Why is it wrong to set limits without helping the youth develop alternatives? _____

_____

(3) Explain why a confrontation sets limits on negative behavior. _____

_____

(4) Give an example of a redirection. _____

_____

(5) Give an example of a closed question. _____

_____

PRACTICAL GUIDELINES

T   F

☐ ☐ 1. Overt aggression is a good reason to initiate a Called Group.

☐ ☐ 2. Distribution of mail is a good reason to initiate a Called Group.

☐ ☐ 3. Any youth may initiate a Called Group.

☐ ☐ 4. A staff can delay the conclusion of a Called Group.

☐ ☐ 5. Ideally, in a Daily Group each youth should report on his/her own problems and successes.

☐ ☐ 6. It is never okay for a group counselor to give a report on a youth.

☐ ☐ 7. The focus of the group session is determined by who most needs the group.

☐ ☐ 8. The problem-solving process of the Daily Group requires youths to identify and accept problems.

☐ ☐ 9. Youths must be able to explain why a behavior is a problem.

☐ ☐ 10. A large part of a Daily Group is connecting the present problem to other problems the youth has had.

☐ ☐ 11. The youth does not need to develop alternatives for problem behavior.

☐ ☐ 12. Seed Groups are used to punish negative behavior.

T   F

□   □   13. When a youth is doing well and exhibiting prosocial behavior, the counselor should use a limit intervention.

□   □   14. Process comments focus on why the group or individual behaves the way he/she does.

□   □   15. Offense Cycle Worksheets are done 30 days prior to leaving the facility.

□   □   16. The Offense Cycle refers to the youth's style and habits of illegal behavior.

□   □   17. Recidivism happens quickly with no warning.

□   □   18. Recidivism can be triggered by negative events.

□   □   19. A trigger is a negative event that can get a youth thinking about doing a crime.

□   □   20. Victim empathy emphasizes that victims cause crimes and are responsible for their own victimization.

CHARACTERISTICS OF DELINQUENT YOUTH

Delinquency is a lifestyle. The more delinquent characteristics possessed by a youth, the more severe the delinquency. Youth with many delinquent characteristics have a life style of exploiting and harming others.

DELINQUENT STRENGTHS

These characteristics enable the youth to take advantage of others:

- *Power play.* Manipulation and domination
- *Fronting.* Secrets and lies
- *Energy.* Mental and physical activity
- *False pride.* Entitlement and ownership
- *Corrosion.* Cannot keep commitments

DELINQUENT WEAKNESSES

These are the positive skills that the delinquent has not developed because the delinquent strengths work too well.

- *Responsibility.* Self-starter who does what is "right"
- *Empathy.* Knows how others feels and considers it before acting
- *Thinking.* Poor learning and memory
- *Counterdependence.* Not independent but not dependent
- *Internal Control.* Cannot tolerate tension

STRENGTH OF ADOLESCENCE

Adolescents possess strengths that enable them to change more readily than adults.

Appendix C

GROUP MONITORING FORM

GROUP MONITORING FORM

Date: _____   Group Monitor: _____

Group Size: _____   Group Meeting Started: _____

                                                   Ended: _____

Group Counselor: _____

PRE-GROUP

- Appropriateness of students for group (proper dress, seating arrangement, setting, and so on)

_____

_____

_____

GROUP MEETING

- Meeting structure and process (group counselor and student adherence to group standards)

_____

_____

_____

- Self-report

_____

_____

_____

- Assigning the focus

_____

_____

_____

- Problem solving

_____

_____

_____

- Conclusion

_____

_____

_____

GROUP COUNSELOR'S TECHNIQUES

- Strengths/weaknesses _____

_____

_____

_____

- Ability to gauge developmental level of group and provide appropriate interventions

_____

_____

_____

- Follow-through with pending past issues _____

_____

_____

_____

- Thoroughness of wrapping up loose ends from meeting _____

_____

_____

_____

- Other comments _____

_____

_____

_____

Appendix D

PERSONAL HISTORY WORKSHEET

PERSONAL HISTORY WORKSHEET

FAMILY

DOB _____   Place of Birth _____

Names of family members   Ages

_____

_____

_____

_____

Description of family members _____

_____

_____

Illegal activities by family members _____

_____

_____

How did these activities affect you? _____

_____

_____

SCHOOL

First school _____

Last school _____

Did your parent prepare you for school? _____

How much school did your parents complete? _____

How much school did your siblings complete? _____

How important was school to your family? _____

What are your personal goals for school? _____

Describe any problems that you encountered at school. _____

_____

_____

PEERS

Who was your first friend? _____

Who are your best friends at home? _____

Do your friends do crimes? _____

Are you comfortable around peers who do not do crimes? _____

How do you pick your friends? What do you look for in a friend? _____

_____

_____

Are your friends part of the reason that you are here? _____

Are you a leader or a follower? _____

DELINQUENT HISTORY

How many times have you been arrested? _____

How many times have you broken the law and not been arrested? _____

Do you enjoy doing crimes? Why? _____

_____

Are you going to do crimes all your life? _____

COMMITTING OFFENSE

What was your committing offense? _____

When and where did it occur? _____

Was it planned? By whom? _____

Were you alone? _____

Who was our victim? _____

What was his/her name? _____

How does your victim feel about what you did? _____
_____

If your victim saw you today, what would he/she say to you? _____
_____

What do your parents think about you now that you are here? _____
_____

How do you feel about being here? _____
_____

Who is to blame for your being here? _____
_____
_____

FUTURE

What are your chances of your committing another crime? _____

What are your chances of being recommitted? _____

What goal do you have for the future? Specify what you must do. _____

    (1) _____

    (2) _____

    (3) _____

    (4) _____

    (5) _____

Do you have any role models? _____

How would it feel to be like them? _____
_____
_____

REFERENCES

Agee, V. L., & McWilliams, B. (1984). The role of group therapy and the therapeutic community in treating the violent juvenile offender. In R. A. Mathias, P. Dumuro, & R. S. Allinson (Eds.), *Violent juvenile offenders: An anthology* (pp. 283-296). San Francisco: National Council on Crime and Delinquency.

Allison, T. L., & Bacon, L. W. (1990). Holding ourselves accountable. *Corrections Today, 52,* 16-20.

American Association of Correctional Psychologists. (1979). *Standards for psychology services in adult prisons and jails.* Beverly Hills, CA: Sage.

American Corrections Association. (1983). *Standards for juvenile training schools* (2nd ed.). Washington, DC: Author.

Andrews, D. A. (1983). Assessment of outcome in correctional samples. In M. J. Lamber, E. R. Christensen, & S. S. DeJulio (Eds.), *Assessment of psychotherapy outcome* (pp. 160-201). New York: John Wiley.

Andrews, D. A., Bonta, J., & Hoge, R. P. (1990). Classification for effective rehabilitation: Rediscovering psychology. *Criminal Justice and Behavior, 17,* 19-52.

Bard, M. & Sangrey, D. (1984). *The crime victim's book.* New York: Brunner/Mazel.

Beutler, L. E., (1979). Toward specific psychological therapies for specific conditions. *Journal of Consulting and Clinical Psychology, 47,* 882-897.

Brentro, L. K., & Ness, A. E. (1982). Perspectives on peer group treatment: The use and abuse of guided group interaction/positive peer culture. *Children and Youth Services Review, 4,* 307-324.

Buss, A. H., & Durkee, A. (1957). An inventory for assessing different kinds of hostility. *Journal of Consulting Psychology, 21,* 343-349.

Davis, R. C. (1984). Crime victims: Learning how to help them. *National Institute of Justice Reports, 203,* 2-7.

Garrett, C. J. (1985). Effects of residential treatment on adjudicated delinquents: A meta-analysis. *Journal of Research in Crime Delinquency, 22,* 287-308.

Gendreau, P. & Ross, R. R. (1987). Revivification of rehabilitation: Evidence from the 1980s. *Justice Quarterly, 4,* 349-408.

Gendreau, P. & Ross, R. R. (1984). Correctional treatment: Some recommendations for effective treatment. *Juvenile and Family Court Journal, 34,* 31-39.

Gendreau, P. & Ross, R. R. (1979). Effective correctional treatment: Bibliotherapy for cynics. *Crime and Delinquency, 25,* 463-489.

Glasser, W. (1965). *Reality therapy.* New York: Harper & Row.

Goldstein, A. P., Glick, B., Riener, S., Zimmerman, D., Coultry, T. M., & Gold, D. (1986). Aggression replacement training: A comprehensive training for the acting-out delinquent. *Journal of Correctional Education, 37,* 120-126.

Goldstein, A. P., & Glick, B. (1987). *Aggression replacement training.* Champaign, IL: Research Press.

Goldstein, A. P., Sprafkin, R. P., Gershaw, N. J., & Klein, P. (1980). *Skillstreaming the adolescent: A structured learning approach to teaching prosocial skills.* Champaign, IL: Research Press.

Gorski, T. T., & Miller, M. (1979). *Counseling for relapse prevention*. Hazel Creek, IL: Alcoholism Systems Associates.

Greer, J. G., & Stuart, I. R. (1983). *The sexual aggressor: Current perspectives on treatment*. New York: Van Nostrand Reinhold.

Harstad, C. D. (1976). Guided group interaction: Positive peer culture. *Child Care Quarterly, 5,* 109-120.

Kazdin, A. E., Enveldf-Dawson, K., French, N. H., & Unis, A. S. (1987). Problem-solving skills training & relationship therapy in the treatment of antisocial child behavior. *Journal of Consulting & Clinical Psychology, 55,* 76-85.

Lab, S. P., & Whitehead, J. T. (1988). An analysis of juvenile correctional treatment. *Crime and Delinquency, 34,* 60-83.

Marlatt, G. A., & Gordon, J. R. (Eds.). (1987). *Relapse prevention*. New York: Guilford Press.

Martinson, R. (1974). What works? Questions and answers about prison reform. *Public Interest, 35,* 22-54.

Maslow, A. H. (1962). Some basic propositions of a growth and self-actualization psychology. *Perceiving, behaving & becoming: A new focus for education*. Yearbook for the association of supervision and curriculum development. Washington, DC.

McCorkle, L. W., Elias, A., & Bixby, F. L. (1958). *The Highfields story*. New York: Holt, Rinehart & Winston.

Meichenbaum, D., & Turk, D. C. (1987). *Facilitating treatment adherence: A practitioners guidebook*. New York: Plenum.

National Commission on Correctional Health Care. (1984). *Standards for health services in juvenile confinement facilities*. Chicago: Author.

National Commission on Correctional Health Care. (1987). *Standards for health services in prisons*. Chicago: Author.

Ollendick, T. H., & Hensen, M. (1979). Social skills training for juvenile delinquents. *Behavior Research & Therapy, 17,* 547-554.

Palmer, T. (1975). Martinson revisited. *Journal of Research in Crime & Delinquency, 12,* 133-152.

Pithers, W. D., Marques, J. K., Gibat, C. C., & Marlatt, G. A. (1983). Relapse prevention with sexual aggressives: A self control model of treatment and maintenance of change. In J. G. Greer & I. R. Stuart (Eds.), *The sexual aggressor: Current perspectives on treatment*. New York: Van Nostrand Reinhold.

Prentky, R. & Burgess, A. W. (1990). Rehabilitation of child molesters: A cost benefit analysis. *American Journal of Orthopsychiatry, 60,* 108-117.

Redl, F., & Wineman, D. (1951). *Children who hate*. New York: Free Press.

Rogers, C. R. (1957). *Client centered therapy*. Dallas: Houghton Mifflin.

Romig, D. A. (1982). *Justice for our children*. Austin: Human Sciences Press.

Ryan, G., Lane, S., Davis, J., & Issac, C. (1987). Juvenile sex offenders: Development and correction. *Child Abuse & Neglect, 11,* 385-395.

Samenow, S. (1984). *Inside the criminal mind*. New York: Times Books.

Sechrest, L. (1987). Classification for treatment. In D. M. Gottfredson & M. F. Tonry (Eds.), *Prediction and classification. Criminal justice decision making*. Chicago: University of Chicago Press.

Sechrest, L., White, S. O., & Brown, E. D. (1979). *The rehabilitation of criminal offenders: Problems and prospects*. Washington, DC: National Academy of Sciences.

Smith, M. L., & Glass, G. V. (1977). Meta-analysis of psychotherapy outcome studies. *American Psychologist, 32,* 752-760.

Stiles, W. B., Shapiro, D. A., & Elliot, R. (1986). Are all psychotherapies equivalent? *American Psychologist, 41,* 165-180.

Truax, C. B., Wargo, D. G., & Volksdorf, F. R. (1970). Antecedents to outcome in group counseling with institutionalized juvenile delinquents. *Journal of Abnormal Psychology, 76,* 235-242.

Vorath, H. H., & Brentro, L. K. (1974). *Positive Peer Culture.* Chicago: Aldine.

Walters, G. D. & White, T. W. (1990). Therapeutic interventions with the lifestyle criminal. *Journal of Offender Counseling, Services and Rehabilitation, 14,* 159-169.

Wayson, B. L., Funk, G. S., & Falkin, G. P. (1984). *Managing correctional resources: Economic analysis techniques.* Washington, DC: National Institute of Justice.

Yalom, I. D. (1975). *The theory and practice of group psychotherapy.* New York: Basic Books.

Yochelson, S., & Samenow, S. (1976). *The criminal personality* (Vols. 1-2). New York: Jason Aronson.

Zamble, E., & Porpornio, F. J. (1988). *Coping, behavior and adaptation in prison inmates.* New York: Springer-Verlag.

ABOUT THE AUTHOR

Matthew L. Ferrara received a doctoral degree in clinical psychology from Oklahoma State University. He began working in corrections as the Chief of Counseling for the Texas Youth Commission (TYC). During his tenure with TYC, he developed a group counseling program, sex offender treatment program, and several programs for special-needs youth, e.g., aggressive youth, arsonists, and low self-esteem youth. Subsequent to his work with TYC, he worked as a unit psychologist and as the Chief Psychologist for the Texas Department of Criminal Justice (TDCJ). While serving as the Chief Psychologist for TDCJ, he developed and implemented two programs: the Sex Offender Treatment Program and the Program for the Aggressive Mentally Ill Offender. He is currently in private practice in Austin, Texas and does contract work with adult and juvenile probation and the county sheriff. He also consults nationwide, offering program development services and training programs.